HOWE & HUMMEL

Howe & Hummel

THEIR TRUE AND SCANDALOUS HISTORY

By Richard H. Rovere

ILLUSTRATED BY REGINALD MARSH

———

WITH AN INTRODUCTION BY

JUDGE JAMES GARRETT WALLACE

NEW YORK · 1947
FARRAR, STRAUS AND COMPANY

This book is an expanded and, to some extent, revised version of four articles that originally appeared in the *New Yorker* under the title 89 Centre Street.

The drawings by Reginald Marsh on pages 22, 52, 96, 142, Copyright, The F-R Publishing Corporation, reproduced by permission of the *New Yorker*.

For my mother
and father

ACKNOWLEDGMENTS

THIS book, like many more imposing works of research, owes its existence to several persons besides the author. Most of those upon whose writings and long memories I have drawn are identified in the text. Others gave me to understand that they would prefer not to be mentioned. Anyway, I am indebted to all of them. I am also grateful for the help I have had from Harold Ross, William Shawn, and Hugh Angleton of the *New Yorker*; Felix E. Larkin and Eugene Nadelman, attorneys and scholars, of New York City, and White Plains, New York, respectively; the writers M. R. Werner and Herbert Asbury; Frederick E. Woltman of the *New York World-Telegram*; Clarence Saunders Brigham of the American Antiquarian Society in Worcester, Massachusetts; and my wife, Eleanor Burgess Rovere.

R. H. R.

Hyde Park, New York

CONTENTS

HOWE & HUMMEL

INTRODUCTION

WHEN I was asked to write the introduction to this very interesting little book, I thought at once, not of courts or lawyers, crimes or criminals, but of Henry Lee.

Henry Lee was an old trouper, a former Shakespearean actor who, in the nineties, gravitated into what Mr. B. F. Keith, of Boston, New York, and points west, called "polite vaudeville." I often caught Henry's act in Keith's Union Square Theatre, on Fourteenth Street, Manhattan. Henry impersonated the great men of his day. He made up right out on the stage, in full view of the audience, but with his back to the foot-lights. He had a complete change of costume for each character, and made the changes very rapidly. Every time he turned around and faced his audience, he was an entirely different character. Henry was a modern Proteus. He would have made a wonderful Presidential candidate.

Now, what brought Henry to mind was not so much what he actually did on the stage, but what he said in introducing his act. When the announcement cards were placed in the racks on either side of the proscenium arch at old Keith's, the piano player would strike a chord, and Henry would emerge from the wings. In long-measured strides, he would take the center of the stage, make a deep bow, draw himself up to full height, and then, in a deep, resonant voice, deliver the following lines:

"Ladies and gentlemen—Introductions are always difficult things to effect; it is so easy to say too much or too little. Then again, we may introduce the wrong people. Today I propose to introduce to you several noted characters—Pope Leo, Prince Bismarck, General Grant, General Lee, Rudyard Kipling and others.

"They will all do their best to please you. Of this I give you my personal assurance. But assurance was always a less marked feature of my character than modesty. Being modest, I am naturally retiring, and as I am retiring, I beg leave to withdraw. Strike up, oh music of the starry spheres, and captive lead our willing, listening ears."

Then Henry would stalk majestically back into the wings, immediately afterward a curtain would rise, and he would be disclosed "going into his act."

Henry was an artist, a headliner in his day. He struck

a responsive chord in my youthful heart, for Henry
was right when he said that introductions are difficult
things to effect. Now, how am I properly to introduce
to the gentle reader of the Atomic Age two fabulous
characters who flourished in the seventies, eighties,
and nineties, and vanished from the local scene early
in the twentieth century?

These glorified shysters, William F. Howe and Abraham Hummel, lived in an era that now seems as remote
as the first Ice Age. They were a part of *their* world
(and underworld). Bon vivants, boulevardiers, bar-
risters extraordinary, they were gems in a setting that
long since has been cast into the crucible of time. They
have no counterparts today. Conditions in our modern
Eden do not favor the flowering of such genius.

In order better to understand these worthies, it will
be well to remember that the world in their day was
much larger than *our* shrunken globe, but that their
city was much smaller, and the minds of its inhabitants
more parochial. Europe, Asia, Africa, Australia, and
South America were just funny-shaped blobs of color
on school maps to many New Yorkers, yes, to most
Americans of that time.

In 1880, New York City had a polyglot population,
nearly a half million of whom could not speak English.
Many could not read or write in any language. New
York, like most eastern seaports, had been flooded by
successive waves of immigration from Ireland, Ger-

many, Italy, and other parts of Europe. The ignorant and illiterate among the newcomers were the natural prey of local political adventurers, and of the predatory of their own races.

This country in the seventies and eighties was just beginning to recover from the effects of the Civil War. The bloody shirt was still being waved, "Secesh, mind your eye," still being sung, and "Johnny Reb" and "Damyankee" were common epithets. The great corner in gold and Black Friday (during Grant's administration), and the financial depredations and brazen skulduggery of Jay Gould, Jim Fiske, and the Erie Railroad gang were recent and juicy scandals.

In 1871, the Tweed Ring was exposed by public-spirited citizens, urged on by *The New York Times* and *Harper's Weekly*, which carried Thomas Nast's devastating cartoons. The City Bar Association was formed to fight the ring. It was led by a valiant fighter for civic decency, Samuel J. Tilden, aided by William M. Evarts, Joseph Choate, and others. The efforts of these and other citizens resulted in the indictment and conviction in 1873 of Tweed, Connolly, and others, the emergence of Tilden as a great political figure, and the election of William L. Strong, a reform mayor, in 1894. Colorful and exciting days these. Corruption then meant actual theft from the public treasury—not using political, financial, or industrial power to levy tribute indirectly in a legalistic, if not legal fashion.

In Howe and Hummel's early days, when you said New York City, you meant the territory now known as Manhattan and the Bronx. Consolidation with Brooklyn and Queens into the Greater City did not take place until 1897. That New York was no city of skyscrapers. The first tall building in our city was the Park Row building at 15 Park Row. The financial district centered around Broad and Wall. Big business institutions in general were located downtown, below City Hall. Maiden Lane was the jewelry center. The big retail dry goods stores were for the most part located on Grand Street, lower Broadway, and lower Sixth Avenue. When you drove up Fifth Avenue toward Forty-second Street you saw many private homes, high-stooped houses of brown or gray stone, and on the left where the Public Library now stands, a grim looking structure, like a redoubt. That was the old reservoir. The Bristol Hotel, a gray stone structure of modest height, stood on the northwest corner of Forty-second and Fifth.

The "Rialto" (theatre district) in the early days centered around Fourteenth Street and Broadway (Union Square). The Morton House, a hotel on the southeast corner of Broadway and Fourteenth Street, was a well-known rendezvous for thespians. With the passing years, the Rialto moved slowly north along the "Main Stem" (Broadway), first to Twenty-third Street, then to Thirty-fourth, and, finally, to Forty-second Street and Broadway (Long Acre Square). Thompson Street, the San Juan Hill section, and Fifty-third Street West, were the colored sections. Harlem, a city in itself, was at that time almost entirely populated by Caucasians.

The streets of New York were largely paved with cobble stones (Belgium blocks). No subways, of course. The first contract to build one was given to John B. McDonald in 1900. Local transportation was by horse-drawn vehicles, including streetcars, and the elevated (steam) railway, with tracks above Second, Third, Sixth, and Ninth Avenues in Manhattan. Then came cable cars, followed by trolleys. In the cable car days, Dead Man's Curve at Fourteenth Street and Broadway, was a place of peril for the unwary. Those really were horse and buggy days. Livery stables instead of garages; smithies instead of auto repair shops; broughams, landaus, surreys, hansom cabs, instead of automobiles and motorcycles. "Brewster" was the hallmark of excellence in vehicles, not Packard, Lincoln, or Cadillac.

And in the good old wintertime, skating in the park, sleigh rides, jingling bells, buffalo robes, sealskin caps, woolen gloves, footwarmers, and cracking whips.

The first driver who sped over the snow to McGowan's Pass Tavern in Central Park won a magnum of champagne, to be drunk on the spot with his party. There were beautiful race-tracks at Morris Park, Sheepshead Bay, and Brighton Beach. Morris Park in particular was noted for the wonderful steeplechases run there, great spectacles in their day.

Most men of the period wore black wool clothing, hard hats, derbies or "high dicers" in the winter, stiff straws in the summer. White shirts with detachable collars and cuffs, studs in the front and open in the back were standard equipment. Cotton, linen, celluloid, and paper collars were in vogue. An old song went:

I wore old paper collars and my salary was ten dollars
Until I wrote Ta, Ra, Ra Boom de aye.

High black shoes were standard for men and women alike. Congress gaiters (shoes with elastic gores in the sides), were popular and were shined with "Bixby's Best Blacking." Some wags asserted that B.B.B. also was used by aging beaux to darken their graying handlebar mustaches.

Low shoes, or Oxford Ties, as they were first called, were rare. And the ladies were protected alike from the elements and the roving male eye by all-enveloping corsets, dresses of dark materials and innumerable petticoats. Their long skirts swept the pavements, unless daintily raised with one or both hands. Women were not publicly acknowledged to be bipeds, although tights were worn on the stage, thanks largely to Howe & Hummel, Mr. Rovere says. Any woman who dared to appear on the beach at Coney Island, Brighton Beach, or Far Rockaway clad in a modern bra-and-diaper combination would first have been mobbed, and then transported to the penitentiary. Blackwell's Island, since renamed Welfare Island by our municipal Nice Nellies, was a summer and winter resort for the erring.

In those days bobbing meant ducking for apples on Halloween, or coursing down a snowy slope on a sled, not getting a haircut. For woman's crowning glory was her lovely long hair. The Seven Sutherland Sisters were pictured on the billboards as shining examples of American womanhood and as visual proof of the value of their marvelous hair tonic. A woman would proudly boast that she could sit on her own luxurious tresses. Well, it kept the ladies out of the barber shop, which, like the old-time club and saloon, still was a refuge from home life.

In the advertisements, babies refused to be happy till they got Pears soap, and children cried for Fletcher's Castoria. So far as is recorded, however, they were not urged to give vent to their desire for "self-expression" by kicking teacher in the shins, or by making nuisances of themselves generally. No, there were no progressive schools.

There were more cigar and pipe smokers, fewer "cigarette fiends." Cigars were cheaper, there were some "twofers," that meant two for a nickel, children, not two for a quarter or half dollar. The horny-handed son of toil smoked Honest Long Cut. It came in a paper package, on the cover of which was the picture of a streetcar driver standing on the front platform of his car, driving his horses and puffing away contentedly on a corncob pipe. A passenger stood beside him on the platform, and issuing from his mouth in a little "balloon," came the slogan, "If that's Honest Long Cut, blow the smoke this way." Some, particularly the younger generation, smoked cigarettes, Sweet Caporal, Jack Rose, Virginia Brights, Richmond Straight Cuts. Little boys loved to collect the "cigarette pictures" that came in every package, pictures of prize fighters, ballplayers, burlesque queens, and other celebrities. Most men considered cigarettes rather effeminate unless the smoker rolled his own with Bull Durham. No ladies, and few women, smoked. Women rarely entered saloons save through the "family entrance," or side door, which led into a restricted cubicle. There they could shove a tin pail (called a growler) through a small window, and wait for their pint of beer to carry home to a thirsty family. This harmless and amiable practice was called "rushing the growler," or "can." Buttering the bottom of the pail discouraged froth, and insured a full pint.

Life was simpler and things were cheaper. Eggs were fifteen cents a dozen, bread five cents a loaf, meat incredibly cheap in the light of present day prices. Your dollar really bought something in those days.

No rationing, no black markets, no traffic or parking problems, in fact no traffic policemen, no autos, no aeroplanes, no rocket-propelled missiles, no atom bomb, no genocide. It was a world fashioned to endure—or so men thought. There were many more morning and evening newspapers in the last three decades of the nineteenth century than there are today, and they were individually owned and controlled. The big newspaper chain, with its standardization of everything from comics to editorials, happily had not been born. There was much less interest in and less coverage of, foreign news. Local items, particularly criminal trials, got a great deal of attention. The tabloid of those days was Richard Kyle Fox's *Police Gazette.*

There were no comic strips but there were dime novels galore. The *Family Story Paper,* with Laura Jean Libbey, *Youth's Companion, The Argosy, St. Nicholas, Frank Leslie's* and *Harper's Weekly* were widely read periodicals. *The Atlantic Monthly* was with us too. Beadle's Dime Library was the daily pabulum of the youngsters. Old Sleuth, Young Sleuth, Old Cap Collier, and Nick Carter were daring detectives of that day, and Frank Reade, Jr., was the Jules Verne of the one-syllable reader. The Shortys, a pair of sadistic young comics, undoubtedly were the spiritual fathers of the Katzenjammer Kids.

"*Life, Puck, Judge,* and *Truth,* Lemon drops, Ridley's peppermints," sang out the "candy butcher" on the Long Island trains as they pulled out of the old "deepo" just across the East River from Thirty-fourth Street, Manhattan. *Life, Puck, Judge,* and *Truth,* all four were humorous weeklies of that day. Two have been transmuted by the alchemy of time into different and baser metal, and two have honorably died.

On the stage, France sent us Bernhardt and Coquelin; Italy, Duse; England, Irving and Terry, E. S. Willard, and many others. Among our local stars were Joe Jeferson, Edwin Booth, the Barretts, the Drews, William H. Crane, Stuart Robson, Ada Rehan—but enough of that, for, since they were mostly Howe & Hummel clients, Mr. Rovere mentions them later on. There was little "canned" music and no radio in those days, but pianos were played in many homes. Folks gathered around them and made their own music. There were good bands—Sousa's, Pryor's, Gilmore's—orchestras, public balls and dances, and the opera for the élite, first in the Academy of Music and later at the Metropolitan.

Then there was the original Madison Square Garden, covering the block from Twenty-sixth to Twenty-seventh Streets between Madison Avenue and Fourth Avenue, a structure with a beautiful tower, a replica of the Campanile. Diana, designed by Saint Gaudens and poised on one toe, adorned the top. The Garden Theatre, a legitimate playhouse, occupied part of the Madison Avenue frontage, and atop the structure was a popular roof garden, on which, one summer evening,

Harry Thaw shot and killed Stanford White, the architect who designed the building.

In the Garden we had the Barnum and Bailey Circus, Buffalo Bill's Wild West Show, championship boxing matches, and games and athletic contests of all kinds. The first six-day bicycle races were held there. The contestants rode high bicycles, and rode until they fell off, exhausted. They had no team mates to relieve them in those days. Teddy Hale, the bearded Irishman, was a winning and popular figure in these races. They were soon prohibited as cruel to the contestants, but when safety bicycles became common, teams of two riders were permitted to compete against other teams, and the races grew in popularity. Among the great riders of that day were Bobby Walthour, Jimmie Michaels, Major Taylor, "Mile-A-Minute" Murphy and Frank Kramer, the king of the sprinters. Bicycles built for two became common on the highways.

In the courts, many lawyers of the first rank appeared for defendants in criminal cases. Practice in the criminal courts was not avoided by the leaders of the Bar, as it is today. The trial lawyer, not the corporation lawyer, was the important figure in those days. The number of corporate clients then available was rather limited.

Among the leading trial lawyers of that day were Willard Bartlett, Tweed's counsel of record and afterwards Judge of the Court of Appeals, John Dos Passos,

Stephen Baldwin of Brooklyn, who was such a dramatic figure that Belasco wanted to make him an actor, Robert M. Moore, Roger Pryor, Ambrose Purdy, DeLancy Nicoll, George Gordon Battle, and James Ridgeway of Brooklyn, a very eloquent gentleman indeed. Then there was Abraham Levy, "The Last Hope," so called because he tried so many difficult cases. The story is told that after the conclusion of a criminal trial in which his client had been convicted, the defendant turned to Counselor Levy and said, "Mr. Levy, what do *we* do now?" To which the learned and benevolent looking counsel for the defense replied, "Well, you're going to jail and I'm going back to my office."

The Court of General Sessions, in which Boss Tweed was indicted in 1871 and convicted in 1873, was the principal court in which Howe and Hummel practiced. In those days, it was called the Court of Oyer and Terminer, meaning a court to hear and determine. Still earlier in its history it had been called the Court of Quarter Sessions. It traces its origin back to the days when New York was an English Crown Colony operating under the Dongan Charter, which took its name from the then Governor of the Colony, Thomas Dongan. In 1870, some Judges of the Court of General Sessions were still called Recorders, a title derived from the early days of the court, when it was part of a Judge's duties to keep a record of various happenings in the old city.

Old New Yorkers will recall Recorders Hackett, Smyth and Goff, whose names struck terror to the hearts of evildoers. Recorder Goff, who afterwards became a Justice of the Supreme Court, and William Travers Jerome, were both Assistants in the New York County District Attorney's Office under District Attorney Fellows.

John W. Goff was a saintly looking old gentleman, with flowing white hair, a white beard, a ruddy complexion, and a soft low voice. In his day, defendants' lawyers who lost cases before him used to claim that when Goff charged the jury, all you could hear him say was, "Buzz, buzz, buzz, guilty, buzz, buzz, guilty, buzz, buzz, buzz, find the defendant guilty." Enough of his charges evidently got into the trial record, for convictions before Judge Goff usually were sustained on appeal.

On January 1st, 1899, Theodore Roosevelt, who had been a candidate for Mayor of the old city in 1886, a Police Commissioner of New York, an Assistant Secretary of the Navy, and Lieutenant Colonel of the Rough Riders in the Spanish-American War, became Governor of New York State. Tom Platt, the "Easy Boss" of the Republican Machine, had nominated him, not that he really wanted "Teddy," but because he needed a strong "soldier candidate" in 1896 to offset the effect of the Erie Canal scandals, in which his party workers were deeply involved.

Colonel Asa Bird Gardiner, a Democrat and a fiery-tempered old soldier, had been elected District Attorney in 1898. Thereafter, in 1900, charges were preferred to the Governor against him, and Roosevelt held lengthy hearings upon them. A Scotch verdict of "not proven" was returned. Following these hearings, the doughty Colonel sent a saucy letter to the Governor, and that irate gentleman promptly removed Gardiner from office. Roosevelt then appointed Eugene A. Philbin, a Democrat and a highly respected lawyer, to fill the vacancy until the 1901 Election. The Mayoralty and other city and county offices were at stake in that Election. A "Fusion" was effected between the Republicans and a number of independent bodies. The Fusionists nominated Seth Low, President of Columbia University, and former Mayor of Brooklyn, as their candidate for Mayor. William Travers Jerome was the Fusion candidate for District Attorney.

For various reasons, but mainly because he was thought to be financially interested in the so-called Ice Trust, Robert A. Van Wyck, in 1897 elected the first Mayor of Greater New York, by 1901 had become extremely unpopular and was denied a renomination for Mayor. The Ice Trust, with the help of Van Wyck and others, had gotten control of all the ice coming into New York City, and like most monopolies, it had raised prices and aroused public resentment. Therefore Croker, the Democratic boss, decided not to renominate Van Wyck. Edwin M. Shephard, a prominent and highly respected lawyer, was nominated for Mayor by the Democrats. Van Wyck was consoled by a nomination for Justice of the Supreme Court. The newspapers whipped up a torrent of feeling against him and urged the Democratic voters to insure his defeat by splitting their tickets. Voting-machines were not in use in 1901. When a voter went to the polls he was handed a paper ballot with the names of the candidates listed on it in party columns. The party emblem appeared at the head of each column: For the Democrats, the Star, for the Republicans, the Eagle. Henry W. Unger was the Democratic candidate for District Attorney, and his name appeared in the Democratic column on the ballot under the names of Shephard and Van Wyck.

Jerome conducted a vigorous campaign and drew to his support many independent voters, as well as the Republican regulars. He distributed square black campaign buttons with "JEROME" printed diagonally across them in white letters, and his campaign slogan was "Jerome on the Square."

Ironically enough, he would have been defeated if Democratic voters·had not inadvertently helped to insure his election. In New York County, thousands of them voted a straight Democratic ticket, except for Van Wyck. His name they either scratched out or defaced by writing scurrilous and indecent comments over it. The ballots so defaced were legally void and could not be counted for any candidate. If all those ballots had not been "spoiled" and thus voided, Henry Unger would have been elected District Attorney; but they were thrown out, and this gave Jerome the victory and the office. If voting-machines had been in use, Unger probably would have won. Yet, Tammany always fought the introduction of the machines.

Thereafter, Jerome prosecuted and convicted Hummel for the crooked work Little Abe did in connection with the Dodge-Morse annulment case. Hummel's client in that case was the man who had interested Van Wyck in the Ice Company, hence the man who indirectly helped to elect Jerome—the organizer of the Ice Trust, Charles W. Morse. Morse was a wily and resourceful scoundrel but he finally got into the toils, was convicted in a Federal Court, and sentenced to a considerable term in prison. While so confined, he ate some jail soap, foamed at the mouth, and got doctors to assert that he had but a short time to live.

An amiable and easily fooled gentleman, William Howard Taft, gave Morse a Presidential pardon. Morse, after his release, changed his diet and lived on serenely and profitably for years. Had he survived until radio broadcasting became profitable and continued his saponaceous suppers, in all likelihood he would have ended his days as a soup salesman or a perfume peddler.

Scalawags scampered blithely and boldly in the limelight in those days (as, indeed, they do in ours), but the vast majority of New Yorkers, then as now, were decent, hard-working folk, who never came into contact with the criminal courts.

True, there were no subways, no bridges over the rivers until the Brooklyn Bridge was opened in 1883, no automobiles, no aeroplanes, no electric trains, no moving pictures, and no radios, and not many asphalted streets, no night clubs, and few publications of the modern kind. But we had no loudspeakers to make the night and day hideous, no Hollywood double features of idiotic content, no radio announcers, feverishly and with high excitement magnifying their mole hills, no singing commercials, no threats of imminent destruction falling from the sky. The pretentious voice of the news commentator, affecting omniscience, and the syrupy saga of the radio salesman, did not filter through your walls in winter or come through your open windows on a summer's evening. One had to walk more, but the exercise was beneficial, and shoes were made of stout leather. Moreover, the city air was fresh and pure, not the dust laden "Pittsburgh Smog" of today. Vigorous appetites could be satisfied with good food at reasonable prices. Instead of the celluloid ghosts of the cinema, with their distorted close-ups and gelatin tears, there were many theatres with real flesh-and-blood actors, and many good vaudeville and variety shows. An orchestra seat in a theatre cost a dollar and a half or two dollars at the box office, and ticket speculators were rare birds. There were some cut-rate seats, too. At Joe Leblang's ticket desk in a cigar store on lower Sixth Avenue the thrifty could buy two lithograph seats (seats distributed to merchants for exhibiting advertising cards in their windows) for a dollar and a half, *two seats in the orchestra!* An oyster stew or an oyster fry after the show was considered by most a sufficient evening repast, when washed down with a glass of beer or a cup of coffee, and in scores of restaurants such a meal could be had for twenty-five cents.

With cocktails at two for a quarter, other drinks proportionately low, and hundreds of stores selling cigars at reasonable prices, life in those days was far from unpleasant. *Our* hucksters peddled fruit and vegetables on the streets, not piffle and propaganda in the press and magazines; the bright boys of advertising and the public relations counselors had not taken over the direction of our "way of life." In fact, folks in those days didn't know they had a "way of life." They just lived.

JAMES GARRETT WALLACE

CHAPTER ONE

HOWE THE LAWYER
AND LITTLE ABE

I N 1891, ten years before the founding of the Hall of Fame on University Heights, the *National Police Gazette*, then at its most popular and prosperous, started a Hall of Fame of its own. It consisted not of bronze busts in a marble colonnade but of photographs, finished in sepia and suitable for framing, which sold for a dime apiece. Its members, numbering about two hundred, were not dead statesmen, inventors, and authors but living prize-fighters, billiard champions, actresses (actresses' photographs were available in three poses: "in costume," "in tights," or "bust showing"), and popular adventurers of one sort or another. The idea of the Hall of Fame was well received by

readers of the *Gazette*, and for years the photographs
were standard items of decoration in pool parlors,
political clubs, and hall bedrooms throughout the
country. It would be instructive to know which of
those enshrined in this proletarian pantheon were most
in demand among the subscribers, but the records, if
any were kept, no longer exist. It is perhaps reasonable,
however to assume that those whose names appeared
at the head of the list in advertisements were the biggest
drawing cards. These were President Harrison and
Queen Victoria; the actresses Lillian Russell, Ada
Rehan, and Lillie Langtry; the pugilists John L. Sullivan and Jake Kilrain; William F. Cody, the Indian
fighter; Steve Brodie, the high-diving tavern keeper;
Fred Taral, the great jockey; and two New York attorneys, William F. Howe and Abraham H. Hummel.

Except for the two representatives of the bar, the
list provides no surprises. Most of its members are still
celebrated. If, looking backward from this era of puny
lawyers, it seems strange that a pair of counselors-at-
law should once have crowded presidents and queens,
prize-fighters and hourglass torsos for space on the
walls of barbershops, saloons, and clerks' lodging-
houses, it seemed anything but strange at the time.
Readers of the *Police Gazette* in the eighties and nineties
were as familiar with the exploits of the Messrs. Howe
and Hummel in cheating justice and, on occasion, in doing poetic justice at the criminal bar as they were with

the exploits of the Boston Strong Boy on the torchlit barges on which he fought or with the adventures of Miss Russell in her search for a durable spouse. Howe and Hummel, partners in Howe & Hummel's Law Offices at 89 Centre Street, New York City, were beyond dispute the greatest criminal lawyers of their day and quite possibly the greatest in American history. William J. Fallon, who is still the cult hero of the profession, was counsel to a hundred and twenty-six defendants in homicide cases; Samuel Leibowitz, before his elevation to the Brooklyn bench, defended a hundred and forty-one; Earl Rogers of Los Angeles, fewer than a hundred; Moman Pruiett, the Oklahoma advocate, three hundred and forty-three; and Abraham Levy, the best-known contemporary of Howe & Hummel, a few more or less than three hundred. Between 1869, when it was organized, and 1907, when it was put out of business by District Attorney William Travers Jerome, the firm of Howe & Hummel defended more than a thousand people indicted for murder or manslaughter, and the senior partner, William F. Howe, himself appeared in behalf of more than six hundred and fifty of them. In that unstatistical period, criminal lawyers did not keep charts and graphs of their acquittals, and it is impossible now to present an audited statement of Howe & Hummel's record. They undoubtedly did all right, though, or they would not have interested the readers of the *Police Gazette*, to say nothing of several hundred citizens facing either the gallows or what in its early days was called the electrical chair.

Howe & Hummel had almost a monopoly on the rest of the criminal business in New York in their day. They were the attorneys for all the major brothel owners. When seventy-four madams were rounded up during a purity drive in 1884, every one of them named Howe & Hummel as counsel. Mother Mandelbaum, the leading fence of the age, paid Howe & Hummel a retainer of five thousand dollars a year to defend her and her army of thieves. The firm had the legal business of General Abe Greenthal's Sheeny Mob, a nationwide syndicate of pickpockets; of Chester McLaughlin's Valentine Gang of forgers; and of the Whyos, an organization of thugs and killers that was perhaps the toughest of all the nineteenth-century gangs. William Mosher, the professional thief, and his partner, Joe Douglas, who confessed, as he lay dying, that he and Mosher were the kidnappers of Charlie Ross, were Howe & Hummel clients. Howe & Hummel represented the Pool Sellers Association, the trade agency of the city's policy-shop owners and bookmakers. Charles O. Brockway, a counterfeiter so adroit that the United States Treasury once had to withdraw an issue of its own hundred-dollar bills because they were indistinguishable from his, found it expedient to pay Howe & Hummel in genuine coin of the realm. It was

Howe & Hummel who collected ninety thousand dollars—said to be the largest fee paid any criminal lawyers before prohibition—from George Leonidas Leslie, alias Western George, and his accomplices in the robbery of the Manhattan Savings Institution in 1878. The two lawyers had in addition the business of every free-lance safecracker, forger, arsonist, confidence man, bucket-shop proprietor, and panel thief whose business was worth having. Howe & Hummel were the mouthpieces—if not, as was often asserted, the brains —of organized crime in New York for more than thirty years. Needless to say, most of these clients bought liberty with their counsel fees.

The New York bar was enjoying a second golden age in the years when Howe & Hummel were practicing. Alexander Hamilton, Chancellor Kent, and John Jay had long been dead, but Joseph Choate, Elihu Root, and the incomparable James T. Brady were appearing regularly in the city's courts. So were J. Hampden Dougherty, Commodore Gerry, Frederic Coudert, Chauncey Depew, De Lancey Nicoll, John B. Stanchfield, Thomas Nolan, and John R. Dos Passos. Toward the end of Howe & Hummel's time, Charles Evans Hughes and William Travers Jerome became illustrious names at the bar. But to the public, Howe & Hummel were better known than any of the rest. They had the cases that made the newspapers, and the newspapers wrote intimately of them, as they did of sports figures and popular politicians. Howe was spoken of as Howe the Lawyer, Hummel as Little Abe. "They were so much a part of the New York scene," Samuel Hopkins Adams, who remembers them from his early days as a newspaper reporter, recalled recently, "that the wiseacre invariably responded to his drinking companion's 'Here's how' with 'Here's Hummel.' " They seemed to be everybody's lawyers. If they had not earned their place in the *Police Gazette's* Hall of Fame in their own right, they would have deserved some sort of honorary recognition as the attorneys and confidants of all of the other members except for a few out-of-towners like President Harrison, Buffalo Bill, and Queen Victoria. They even represented the *Gazette* itself and its publisher, Richard Kyle Fox. When John L. Sullivan and Alf Greenfield, the challenging British heavyweight champion, were indicted for "fighting without weapons" (prize-fighting was then illegal) in Madison Square Garden in 1884, they were defended by Howe & Hummel, who won an acquittal that did much to give "demonstrations of scientific skill in sparring" a legal standing in this state. They were attorneys for Caleb Mitchell and Peter De Lacey, the most famous gamblers in the country, next to Richard Canfield; for Alice Jennings, the champion lady boxer; and for Theodore Allen, the owner of the infamous St. Bernard Hotel, at Prince

and Mercer Streets, who was known to the newspapers
as The Allen, the Wickedest Man in New York.

The firm's practice in the civil courts and the courts
of equity was almost as extensive as its criminal practice. Bankers, brokers, actors, and society women
jostled jostlers and banco men in the waiting room of
Howe & Hummel's. "It was not rare," Theron G.
Strong wrote, in *Landmarks of a Lawyer's Lifetime*,
"that a dozen carriages of the wealthier class were
gathered in the street in front of [their] office." The
carriage trade came mostly to get, or prevent, divorces.
Howe & Hummel were pre-eminent among divorce
lawyers. They were also the leading theatrical lawyers.
Scarcely anyone of consequence in the entertainment
world did not entrust his fortunes, personal and professional, to Howe & Hummel. Among the firm's
theatrical clientele were P. T. Barnum, Edwin Booth,
Sir Henry Irving, Fay Templeton, Ned Harrigan,
Tony Pastor, Agnes Ethel, George Lederer, John
Drew, John Barrymore, Charles and Daniel Frohman,
Ada Rehan, Little Egypt, Lester Wallack, Mary An-
derson, Nat Goodwin, and Lillie Langtry. When
Barnum, a prohibitionist of strong conviction, wanted
contracts that would effectively enjoin the midgets and
the dog-faced boys from ever using alcohol, Howe
& Hummel, who had nothing against virtue when it
paid, drew them for him, and when Olga Nethersole,
playing the title role in Daudet's *Sapho*, got arrested

for publicly demonstrating the smoky embrace known as "the Nethersole kiss," Howe & Hummel explained to the court that Miss Nethersole had given art a new dimension. The court agreed. The firm's theatrical practice was the only respectable part of its practice. No member of the American bar knew more about dramatic rights and contracts than Hummel, and some of his briefs, cribbed by judges for their opinions, are today part of the law as it applies to the theatre. The firm did a moderate amount of business in wills, trusts, taxes, and estates, but the partners found the paper work that this entailed dull. They took jobs of this sort mostly as a convenience for the more affluent members of their criminal and theatrical clientele, and they hired competent underlings to handle the details.

It might be said that Howe & Hummel were the classic shysters. The term "shyster" appears to have originated in New York, having derived, according to the findings in a recent philological inquiry, from the name of a certain Attorney Scheuster, pronounced "Shoister," who, back around 1840 or 1845, so vexed Justice Osborne of the Essex Market Police Court that the bench took to rebuking other lawyers for "Scheuster practices." Counselor Scheuster may have been a formidable pettifogger and judge-baiter, but he will be remembered, if at all, only as an eponym. Court records unquestionably contain mentions of him, but he did nothing to impress the newspapers. His

name is nowhere to be found in their indexes. Howe
& Hummel, on the other hand, are still spoken of by
cops and lawyers, police reporters and court attendants
along Centre Street with the same respect for dead
giants that other people show for Sarah Bernhardt,
Christy Matthewson, Charlie Murphy, and Zev. Their
hoaxing of juries, their inspired quibbling, and their
skill in fabricating evidence are part of the bar's folklore. Little Abe Hummel's fight against William
Travers Jerome for professional survival, which lasted
from 1903 to 1907, is still considered one of the country's classic legal struggles. Howe & Hummel found
loopholes large enough for convicted murderers to
walk through standing up. Once, in 1888, Howe produced a state of terror in the city by invoking a tech-
nicality, which, if it had been allowed by the higher
courts, would have set free not only the murderer he
was defending but every other first-degree murderer
then awaiting execution and every defendant then
awaiting trial for first-degree murder. On another occasion, Hummel almost depopulated the city prison
on Blackwell's Island by discovering a technical error
in the procedure by which two hundred and forty
petty criminals had been committed. After collecting a
small fee from each man, they obtained the release of the
entire group. Only sixty-some-odd prisoners were left
on the Island. During the investigation of Judge Albert
Cardozo, the most villainous of the Tweed Ring judges

who were forced from the bench in 1872, it was revealed that he had received bribes to spring more than two hundred Howe & Hummel clients from prison. What expedient the two lawyers—particularly Howe, who seems to have passed the bribes in this instance —used to escape disbarment for this was never known. Possibly one more judge was bribed. A few years later, Hummel actually was disbarred, for attempting to bribe a judge in Westchester, but he was reinstated a month or two later through methods that William Travers Jerome, thirty years afterward, found "too sordid even to discuss." In a short while, Howe was disbarred for the same offense, but he too was reinstated, eight months later. On still another occasion, it was discovered that the firm had represented both the plaintiff and the defendant in a civil suit. No action was taken against the partners, because August Belmont, the victim of the collusion, and his attorney, Joseph Auerbach, who tells the story in *The Bar of Other Days* learned that Benjamin Steinhardt, the Howe & Hummel assistant who had handled the matter, was crippled by locomotor ataxia and had only a short while to live.

Lord Bryce, discussing the bar in the third edition of *The American Commonwealth* in 1893, said that $250,000 was, as far as he knew, the largest annual income of any American law firm. He was never very well acquainted in the Centre Street bar, whose best-known members were generally assumed to be taking in $300,000 or better a year. Ambulance chasing of the usual sort would be beneath the dignity of so prosperous a firm, but it did employ men to collect and collate backstage gossip along Broadway and the Bowery as material for breach-of-promise actions. Breach-of-promise blackmail was a Howe & Hummel specialty, and Howe & Hummel affidavits alleging "seduction under promise of marriage" troubled the morning-after thoughts of playboys and stage-struck businessmen for a quarter of a century. "Deep terror struck the heart of anyone who found Howe & Hummel stationery in his morning mail," George Buchanan Fife once wrote. "An invitation to call at the offices of Howe & Hummel," the late Arthur Train said, "usually brought the recipient running at full speed and bathed in perspiration." It cost anywhere from five to ten thousand dollars to redeem a Howe & Hummel affidavit; the heart balm was split fifty-fifty between the injured lady and her attorneys. Howe & Hummel's process servers and gumshoe men were a highly trained espionage and counter-intelligence unit. The process servers often turned up disguised as Western Union messengers, scrubwomen, and milkmen. A favorite way of delivering a notice of judgment was to have the server pose as a man who had lost his way or was in desperate need of a drink of water. After being admitted to the victim's premises, he would hang around a while, so that the victim would be sure to remember him later on, and surreptitiously plant the notice in a desk drawer or between the pages of some handy book. When the time was up and the adjudged complained that he had never been notified of the action against him, Howe & Hummel would confront him, in court, with the lost or thirsty stranger. The victim would betray the fact that he recognized the man. If he still insisted that no papers had been served on him, Howe & Hummel would suggest that the court authorize a search of his home or office. The papers would be found in the drawer or book.

In the line of professional witnesses, Howe & Hummel kept on call as many sweet-faced grannies, fond wives, doting children, true-blue friends, and chin-choppered family doctors as any Broadway casting agency. The convention against lawyers advertising their services was as firm then as it is now. Howe & Hummel disregarded it. Over their shabby but conspicuous offices on the ground floor of a three-story, red-brick, mansard-roofed building at the southwest corner of Leonard and Centre Streets, across the way from the Tombs, hung not the modest shingle of a firm of counselors-at-law but a sign thirty or forty feet long and three or four feet high with enormous block letters spelling out "Howe & Hummel's Law Offices." It caught the eye of anyone in the vicinity. Illuminated by night, it shone as a beacon of hope and a portent of imminent rescue to prisoners in the Tombs, of whom those who could not afford to retain Howe & Hummel kept their families and friends on the hop trying to round up the necessary cash. Often, when Counselor Howe, who did most of the firm's criminal-trial work, made a particularly brilliant defense of a particularly guilty client, the firm printed the minutes of the trial or the newspaper accounts as a pamphlet and distributed it through the underworld "with the compliments of Howe & Hummel's Law Offices, 89 Centre Street, directly across from Tombs Prison." The partners even advertised the kind of results they got in their cable address, which was LENIENT.

It was said that Howe & Hummel owned reporters on several of the newspapers. Most likely they did. They may have owned publishers too. Herbert Bayard Swope and William O. Inglis, both of the old *World*, are authorities for the statement that Nicholas Biddle, a *Herald* reporter who may or may not have been a descendant of the great banker but who was noted among newspapermen for dressing as elegantly as half a dozen Biddles and for carrying a gold-headed cane to fires and riots, augmented his salary from the paper with one hundred dollars a week from Howe & Hummel. It is certainly true that the firm got its best publicity in the *Herald*, which in the days of the younger James Gordon Bennett reported even the minor Howe & Hummel cases in detail and published the lawyers' literary efforts on such subjects as "Is Love Avoidable?," "Jack the Ripper Explained," "Should the Anti-Tights Law Be Repealed?," "Is Marriage a Failure?," and "Can Lawyers Be Honest?" (They thought that lawyers certainly could be honest.) Any reader of the *Herald*, a paper which offered the unusual service of brothel advertisements, who engaged a firm other than Howe & Hummel was surely aware that he was getting second best. The paper seldom failed to describe Howe as "the Nestor of the Criminal Bar," and it frequently asserted that such-and-such a client's chances of acquittal had "improved considerably when it became known that he had retained the services of the Messrs. Howe & Hummel." It would not be unreasonable to suppose that, in part at least, the *Herald*'s generosity had something to do with legal services rendered the editor-and-publisher. Bennett was constantly getting into the kind of scrape that Howe & Hummel specialized in getting clients out of (and wealthy non-clients into), and if he did not retain Howe & Hummel, he was ignoring the advice of his own paper.

Howe and Hummel were as raffish a pair as any of their clients. Howe was, in the prime of his long career at the bar, a man of enormous frame and girth, deep-chested and lion-headed, with a quantity of wavy gray hair, walrus mustaches, and a ruddy alcoholic complexion. He looked rather like William Howard Taft, and he could have affected great respectability had it not been for his diamonds and his loud, eccentric dress. He had the passion of a Raffles for diamonds. "I started wearing them as a young lawyer," he once explained to a friend, "to show people that I was prosperous. In those days, in New York, no one would have considered hiring a trial lawyer who didn't sport a few diamonds. I really didn't care much for them then, but now I love them. I love the light they throw. I can't get enough of them." He wore diamonds on his fingers, on his watch chains, as shirt studs, and as cuff buttons. He wore neckties only on occasions, such as funerals and hangings, when they were unavoidably *de rigueur*. In place of a tie, he generally wore one of a number of diamond clusters from his large collection. "Lawyer Howe swept into view just in time," the *Herald* once reported. "An entirely new set of studs, pins, and buttons twinkled on a shirt front that was a wonder of brown patterns. A clover leaf with white, pink, and black pearls held a diamond dewdrop between the points of his collar, and an immense diamond fob hung from the gold chain across his ample chest." Dress was an important adjunct of Howe's courtroom technique, and he had several changes of costume, each designed for a definite legal purpose. A customary street attire was trousers with checks of black and white or brown and white, a white doeskin or pearl-gray velvet waist-

coat, and a suit coat of royal purple. He never wore
the stovepipe or beaver hats considered a regulation
part of the lawyer's regalia, wearing instead, in cold
weather or warm, a gold-braided, leather-visored yacht-
ing cap. In summer the crown was white; in winter it
was blue. The various and incongruent elements that
contributed to Howe's appearance made it difficult to
describe him except in rather incongruous terms. Arthur Train said that he looked like a cross between a
Coney Island barker and a costermonger; Joseph Auerbach thought that an outcast of Poker Flat and an
English bookie might convey the proper impression.

As partners should be, Howe and Hummel were
opposites. Howe was big and flamboyant; Hummel
was small and owlish. Hummel, who was twenty-one
years younger than Howe, seems to have been molded
by the gods to play his partner's stooge and Sancho
Panza, the role to which he was invariably assigned
during the first ten or fifteen years of the partnership.
"As Lawyer Howe parried each question with a jest,"
the *Herald* said, in an interview with the partners the
day after Mother Mandelbaum, finally trapped by a
reform district attorney, jumped her bail and fled to
Canada, "the diminutive Lawyer Hummel, from his
perch above a molasses barrel, would put his finger to
his puffed-out cheek and chuckle 'te-he-he,' an expression, it seemed, of admiration for his brilliant partner. 'Too true, too true,' quoth he when Lawyer Howe

would make some apt remark on the points of law involved in the case." Hummel was five feet tall or a
shade under. He had a huge head, which was pear-
shaped, bald, and generally covered by a derby. Although he was runty rather than deformed, he often
left people with the impression that he was a hunch-
back. He had a black mustache, more closely cropped
than Howe's, shifty black eyes, and an unchangingly
noncommittal expression. He complemented Howe in
temperament and manner as much as in appearance.
Howe was a ponderous though forceful man, mentally
as well as physically; Hummel was quick and fussy and
crafty. Howe was coarse and expansive; Hummel was
sleek and foxy. He conformed better than Howe to
the literary stereotype of the shyster. He was, in point
of fact, the model for the protagonist in at least two of
the few attempts that have been made to deal with the
crooked lawyer in American fiction. He is Quibble in
Arthur Train's *Confessions of Artemas Quibble* and
Ambie in Thomas MacMorrow's *Little Ambie* stories.
Bayard Veiller once said that all the lawyers in his
courtroom plays—such as *Within the Law* and *The
Trial of Mary Dugan*—owe something to both Howe
and Hummel, whom he knew in his youth. Hummel
always wore black ensembles, probably to highlight
his partner's gorgeous outfits, and he wore sharply
pointed patent leather shoes, called "toothpick shoes"
by most of the reporters who described them, with

pre-Adler elevator heels. Though sombre, his dress was conspicuously neat, and he was always proud of how tidy and cleanly he was. "I guess that most of what they say about me is true," he told Samuel Hopkins Adams when Jerome was after him. "I'm a crook and I'm a blackmailer. But there's one thing about me—I'm a neat son-of-a-bitch." The sobriety of Hummel's costumes was relieved by a certain amount of precious stones, and although he did not have Howe's lust for diamonds, he was himself a reasonably bejeweled attorney. On the same day that the *Herald* had Howe sweeping into view just in time, "Lawyer Hummel trotted briskly along at his side, a black sprite with little black legs. In the corridors, his diamond-studded matchbox was much in evidence, and a death's-head with diamond eyes grinned from his watch chain."

Many people, among them Arthur Train, who devoted most of his life to a study of crime and criminal law in New York, believed that Howe & Hummel were the master minds of organized crime in their day. It is more likely than not that they counseled clients in the commission of crime as well as in its legal defense, but little positive evidence has ever been assembled to show that they directed criminal operations on a large scale, and it is now a bit late in the day for profitable speculation. It is plain, though, from what records exist that they were both men of criminal instincts. Judge-fixing and subornation of perjury were proved against them in open court, and their work as black-mailers was so well known at the time that they never bothered to take offense at the jokes about it. Either partner, apparently, could turn a hand to crime when prodded by necessity or by want of amusement. Hummel was regarded as an accomplished amateur pick-pocket, and Howe, who had spent most of his early life in England, arrived in this country in 1858 as a ticket-of-leave man, that is, as a paroled convict. The nature of Howe's offense was never made public in this country, but it was often asserted, and not contradicted by him, that he had been a doctor in London and that he had lost his right to practice there as the result of some criminal act. It was also said that before starting his legal practice in New York, he had worked in various American cities as a confidence man and that he was, in fact, either the inventor or the importer of the "sick engineer" game, one of the most successful sucker traps of the period. A New York lawyer of today who as a young man was familiar with the af-fairs of Howe & Hummel remembers that Howe got considerable amusement from trying out various dead-beat tricks on his creditors. "I don't think he ever paid full price for those diamonds of his," this man recalls. "He never bought two at the same jeweler's. When he got one, he would make a small down payment, and then, when he had been dunned two or three times for the balance, he would assign some young shyster in the office to fight the claim. Of course, he had enough money to pay, but he got a kick out of not paying, and he used to say that it was good training for the young fellows to learn to fight claims like that." Howe was very proud of his younger partner's ability as a fork. "Don't you think it's strange?" he once asked his Boswell on the *Herald*. "Abie and I have been going out to the races every fine afternoon this summer. On the way out we sit together on the streetcar and study the forms. We decide which horses we'll bet on and how much we will venture. We place our bets together and stay together most of the afternoon. Yet often, on the way back, I have no money at all and Abie has a thick roll. Honestly, sir, I don't know how he does it."

If Howe & Hummel did play Arnold Rothstein to the underworld of their era, they did so in a far less intense and single-minded fashion than the man Bill Fallon liked to call Ole Massa Mind. Both of them loved travel and high life. They often abandoned their offices for long days at the race tracks, for generous vacations at Saratoga or Long Beach, and for leisurely trips abroad. Howe, who was a family man and appears to have led a sedate enough domestic life, owned a sizable art collection and what was considered, by society reporters at any rate, to be one of the most elegant broughams in the city, and he enjoyed riding in it through the parks, showing off his purple coats and his handsome daughter, an only child. Hummel, a bachelor, was the city's sturdiest first-nighter. "Neither of the partners could be found yesterday morning," the *Herald* once said. "It was learned that Mr. Howe had slipped off to Paris a few days ago, and Mr. Hummel was leading a party of theatre-lovers to Baltimore for the opening of Mr. Fitch's new play." The *Herald* man, incidentally, had stopped by the offices that morning in regard to an interesting client, El Señor Don Julio Campo Serrano, a brigadier general in the Army of the Republic of Colombia who, a week or so before, had been convicted of robbing the corpse of his murdered landlady in a Twenty-third Street boarding-house; but neither the *Herald* man nor any other historian, unfortunately, set down any details of the case.

When Howe and Hummel were on hand, they conducted a large part of their business more or less al fresco. Their ground-floor offices were in a converted store on the site of which there is now a Department of Hospitals clinic. The reception room opened onto the street, and passers-by could measure the volume of business or make a quick survey of local crime conditions by counting the waiting clients, all clearly visible and distinguishable through the plate-glass windows. The illuminated sign over the windows was not considered enough; the windows on either side of the door also bore the partners' names in large letters, and so did two rounded columns that framed the entrance. Old storage rooms opened to the right and left of the reception room. These served as offices for clerks, runners, private detectives, junior partners, and whatnot. Howe & Hummel generally employed about a dozen men in addition to the proprietors, and of these about half were lawyers.

The principals of the firm had adjoining offices at the rear of the building. It is posterity's loss that no one left a fully satisfying account of how these were furnished. Apparently, Howe's office had a molasses barrel that served as a kind of crow's nest for Hummel. When Evelyn Nesbit Thaw was on the witness stand at the trial of her husband for the murder of Stanford White, who was a Howe & Hummel client for many years, she testified that the walls of Hummel's office, which she had once visited to make out an affidavit, were covered with affectionately inscribed portraits of stage beauties. Hummel's office also contained an iron brazier, which was used principally for burning, in the presence of blackmail victims or their attorneys, the legal papers which they had come to the office to ransom. The reception room in the front is said to have been as bare and dingy as a country depot. Howe & Hummel ran a law office, not a cocktail lounge. The seats were splintery wooden benches set with their backs to the walls. A potbellied stove stood in the center and not far from it was a huge safe. The safe never contained anything more negotiable than a coal scuttle. "As recently as 1898," according to a contemporary article on Howe & Hummel, "waiting clients on winter days were frequently astonished to see an office boy make a rush at the old safe, spin its combination lock deftly, throw open its ponderous doors, take from its yawning insides an antique coal bucket, and dump its contents into a large stove that stood in the middle of the room."

Waiting clients must have been frequently astonished by a good many things they saw at Howe & Hummel's. It seems to have been fairly common practice for prisoners who escaped from the Tombs to head straight for the offices of their lawyers, where a skeleton force was on hand all night, and to proceed from there to the next hideaway. Danny Driscoll, the leader of the Whyos, once came running into the office brandishing a knife and oozing blood from several bullet wounds. He was caught later on, and it was subsequently charged, though never proved, that the knife with which he had hacked his way out of prison, cutting up several guards as he moved along, had been supplied him by an employee of Howe & Hummel, who had visited his cell ostensibly to discuss his defense. William J. Sharkey, who made the most notable of all escapes from the Tombs, stopped off at Howe & Hummel's to discard the black wool dress, green veil, and Alpine hat in which he had made his getaway. Sharkey, an ex-pickpocket and a Tammany district leader at the time he killed a gambling companion, was never caught. He finally got to Ireland and lived the rest of his life there. Maggie Jourdan and Mrs. Wesley Allan, the two women who had supplied him with the change of clothes in prison, were both caught, however. They retained Howe & Hummel. Mrs. Allan was not even indicted and Miss Jourdan was acquitted by a jury which agreed with Howe that she had done no more than any red-blooded American woman would do for the man she loved. There was excitement of sorts in the office even when escaped prisoners were not supplying it. The place was a nest of practical jokers. According to a still active attorney who started as an office boy with Howe & Hummel, their establishment was one in which buckets of water could be expected to tip from any transom and chairs were being constantly yanked out from under anyone who tried to sit down on them. "You couldn't say it was a dull place to work," this man recalls. "The lawyers there were always serving one another with fake papers, and every morning when I went to my desk I had to look underneath to see that there wasn't any glue there. Someone was always glueing my shoes to the floor so that when Mr. Howe called me I couldn't move. Howe always thought that was very funny."

No money was ever kept in the Howe & Hummel offices. This was probably a sound business policy in view of the class of people who frequented the place. Numbering so many gifted forgers among their clients, the partners would not accept checks. Payment had to be made in advance and in strictly legal tender. At the close of each day, the two attorneys met at Pontin's Restaurant on Franklin Street, a place devoted mainly to serving the better-paid members of the criminal bar and judiciary, and emptied their pockets on the table. The day's take was divided evenly between the two. Pontin's, incidentally, was like the Stork Club. It had one dining room for the ordinary élite and a special dining room in the rear for the more élite élite. The back room had two tables in it—one for the judges of the Court of General Sessions and one for Howe & Hummel. All of Howe & Hummel's bookkeeping was done on Pontin's tablecloths. The firm kept no account books, and it was shy on records of any sort. There was method in this apparent lack of method. When District Attorney Jerome, investigating the firm's part in the Dodge-Morse divorce scandal in 1905, the case which finally resulted in the imprisonment of Abe Hummel and the dissolution of the firm, subpoenaed the firm's records, he found that there were none. There was not a single item of correspondence, not a single check, not a receipt, not a telegram relating to the case. They had not been destroyed; they had never existed. Howe & Hummel had no use for paper of any kind, except paper money. All their communication with clients was by word of mouth, directly or by telephone, and by messenger. Although the Dodge-Morse case extended in time from 1901 to 1905 and in space, literally, from Maine to Texas, there were no paper records of it whatever. In the absence of account books and annotated Pontin's tablecloths, it is difficult to say what it cost to be a Howe & Hummel client, but it is plain that it cost plenty and that the partners were men of vision in fiscal matters. John L. Sullivan told one of his biographers that he had paid his entire winnings on the Greenfield fight, which drew the largest gate of the decade, to get Howe & Hummel to defend him in the litigation that followed it. The high cost of Howe & Hummel defense was the subject of filler jokes in the newspapers:

> SPOOK OF JUDAS ISCARIOT: Oh why, oh why, couldn't I have had H—e and H-m—l to speak for me?
> MEDIUM: Say, for your measly old thirty plunks you couldn't even have retained Joe Moss.

(Joseph Moss was an assistant to Howe in criminal trials and the manager of the Howe & Hummel road company, which appeared in the provincial courts for persons who wanted the firm's prestige but whose cases were not important enough to induce either partner to leave New York. Moss later became a judge of Special Sessions.)

In the course of being interviewed by the *Herald* on Mother Mandelbaum's bail-hopping, Howe and Hummel were asked if she had left town without settling her account with them. Howe replied, according to the story, by looking "toward the ceiling and jingling some silver in his pocket. Lawyer Hummel, also looking heavenward, softly hummed a tune." The reporter, one of the more impertinent men in the history of his impertinent profession, wrote that he had seen a scratchpad on Howe's desk bearing such notations as "fair divvy . . . my share . . . whack up the real estate." "Real estate" meant, presumably, the hot property which Mother Mandelbaum, who did so large a business that she kept about twenty thieves on a drawing account, had left behind. Neither Howe nor Hummel would say what arrangements they had made with their vanished client, but Howe, in discussing the general question of retainers, said: "We always look ahead. When we take a case, we secure fees covering even an appeal to the Court of Appeals. If our client dies before the appeal is granted, he will never need the money and we might as well have it. If it does go to the higher court, we are secured for our trouble. We look far ahead. We look much further ahead, I may say, than the District Attorney."

The extent of Howe & Hummel's foresight in the

Mother Mandelbaum case was subsequently revealed. When the court demanded forfeiture of her bail, it was found that this could not be arranged. Her lawyers had transferred all the property pledged for her appearance by means of back-dated instruments, and they had shifted all her personal holdings to her daughter. Though it was believed that she made occasional undercover trips to New York, Mother Mandelbaum made Canada her home for the rest of her days.

The partners liked the rustle of bills and the jingle of silver, but they could be munificent at times, particularly at times when charity and self-advertising could walk hand in hand. Sometimes they would defend a deserving client for nothing. "Howe & Hummel," the *Herald* once said, in reporting one such case, "do many similar kindnesses which ne'er reach the ears of the public." This was hyperbole, of course, for the *Herald* always saw that they did reach the ears of the public. Once the *Herald* worked up a column and a half of crocodile tears about the arrest of a bank teller who had pilfered a few dollars to pay the rent for his widowed mother. The paper wanted to know what was to become of justice when this unfortunate and penniless lad could find no lawyer to take his case. Howe & Hummel rushed to his aid and the *Herald* got another column out of that, a report of a talk between the boy's mother and the philanthropic lawyers. "But—but—but what will the fee be?" the mother was said to have asked Howe, who replied: "Don't talk of the sum, dear madam. Don't talk about mere dollars and cents in a case of this kind. Do you think we have no feelings, no sympathies, no hearts? We live in a corner here overspread, so to speak, by the shadow of criminality, but madam, we have our feelings. Haven't we, Abie?" Hummel nodded briskly in agreement. It was left to the *Times* to report, around the same time, that a murderer in the Tombs had been turned down by Howe & Hummel because he could not raise the five thousand dollars they had asked for his defense.

CHAPTER TWO

THE WEEPER

THOSE who took the Master Mind view of Howe and Hummel—that is, those who thought that the partners were the brains of New York's underworld as well as its favorite attorneys—seem generally to have taken it for granted that Hummel was the truly malevolent influence in the firm. "Who," Arthur Train once wrote, "could accomplish that in which the law was powerless?—Hummel. Who could drive to the uttermost ends of this earth persons against whom not a shadow of suspicion had previously rested?—Hummel. Who dictated to chiefs of police in foreign cities what they could and could not do in certain cases? Who could, at the beckoning of his little finger, summon to his dungeon-like offices the most eminent of citizens?—surely none but Hummel. A whisper from

Hummel was enough to make the dry bones of many a powerful and ostensibly respectable official rattle and his tongue cleave to the roof of his mouth in terror."

Besides being unflattering to Lawyer Howe, this parcel of Train rhetoric is plainly too dramatic and romantic a statement of the case against either partner or both combined. Individually and corporately, Howe & Hummel were as crooked as the horns of a Dorset ram. Blackmail, subornation of perjury, the corruption of public officials, and the fabrication of evidence were part of each day's routine in the musty and disordered offices at 89 Centre. But, aside from the fact that some-one in the firm once bribed the constable in a Mexican border town, there is no evidence that they ever insti-gated corruption on a global scale. It is easy to see, though, why Little Abe Hummel should have been considered the evil genius in the firm. For one thing, he looked the part. The bluff and chesty Howe, with his heavy freight of sparklers, his loud clothes, and his bluster, looked rascally enough, but it would be difficult to see him as Mephistopheles. Hummel, on the other hand, with his grotesque little body, his Quasimodo skull, his funereal clothes, and the death's-head watch charm, was easily cast as a man with a direct wire to the kingdom underneath. Whatever its literary convenience, however, this view of Hummel as the baser of the partners seems, in retrospect, to be just one more example of the deceptiveness of outward

things. Hummel had the aspect and the trappings of
the sinister, but many of his intimates remember him
as a cheerful and rather gracious little man, amiable
sometimes to the point of giddiness, whose chief desire
in life was to get along well in the polite race-track
and theatrical society which he found congenial. His
crookedness was of a tidy, business-like sort. It consisted mainly of following the prevailing ethical codes
of his profession to their logical conclusions. Some
people, of a less romantic turn of mind than Arthur
Train, found Hummel easy to like.

If there was really a dark and sinister member of
the firm of Howe & Hummel, it was not Hummel but
Howe. Howe, the great courtroom advocate, the lawyer whom Judge Alton B. Parker called "the father
of the criminal bar in America," was a very queer tick
indeed. He was a man with a past which he found it
prudent to conceal, even to the point of obscuring his
origins. He was always as frank as could be expected
in telling the press about his cases and about the business of the firm, but he rarely provided reporters with
autobiographical data. He kept even his friends in the
dark. "For some reason which I am unable to explain,"
wrote Theron G. Strong, a friend and admirer of
Howe's, in *Landmarks of a Lawyer's Lifetime*, "it was
impossible to induce him to dwell on the experiences
of his early years." The details he did give out were
confused and contradictory. On some occasions, when

pressed for the facts by diligent journalists, he said that he was British by birth and parentage, on others that he was born in or near Boston in 1828 and that "my father was the Rev. Samuel Howe, M.A., a rather well-known and popular Episcopalian clergyman at the Hub in those days." The Boston story turned up more often, but it appears to be the less likely of the two. For one thing, the details changed with each telling. Howe said variously that he was born in Cambridge, on Shawmut Street in Boston, and "in a small village outside the city." The story of his father's ministry is constant but almost palpably untrue. Boston city directories for the 1820's list only two Samuel Howes, the one a musician and the other a boarding-house keeper. (The musician has rather a promising sound.) The Massachusetts Diocese of the Protestant Episcopal Church has no records of any clergymen named Samuel Howe in or around Boston at or around 1828.

Whether William F. Howe was British or American by birth, it is certain that he spent his early years in England, probably in London. The Cockney in his speech never entirely disappeared. "Even when pleading," Samuel Hopkins Adams recalls, "his h's were unreliable." Howe referred often, with pride, to his British upbringing but never with any useful details. He left no clue as to how the son of a Boston minister happened to grow up with a Cockney accent or why a London Cockney should find it advantageous to claim descent from a New England divine. What his life in England was like, whether he lived in good circumstances or poor, and what sort of early schooling he had, he never revealed. In fact, the one time he ever referred in print to his early years, he said that his only vivid childhood recollections were of homicide. These, however, were vivid in the extreme. "My youthful reminiscences of events," he once wrote, in a highly flattering essay about himself, "which happened and of which I heard or read in my youth are chaotic and incongruous, but it is quite otherwise with the murders. I remember with what thrilling interest I read the story of Greenacre, who cut up the body of his victim, carrying the head wrapped up in a handkerchief on his knees in the omnibus and who was supposed nearly to have fainted with fright when, on asking the conductor the fare, received the answer, 'Sixpence a *head*!' Then there was the horrible Dan'l Good, the coachman at Roehampton, and the monster Courvoisier, the Swiss valet, who murdered his master, Lord William Russell, and . . ." Howe, whose interest in violent death always seemed excessive even for a murder lawyer, went on to speak of a number of other garrotings and decapitations that had captured his boyish fancy, but he said nothing about his own doings.

Something more than a bookish interest in crime was responsible for Howe's arrival in New York, in

1858, as a ticket-of-leave man. It is known that Howe had a criminal record at home and the nature of it must have been known to some of the authorities here, but even newspapermen and his fellow-lawyers had no idea what he had actually done. The most commonly advanced theory, according to George Gordon Battle and Terence McManus, who were Assistant New York District Attorneys in the nineties, was that his crime had something to do with the practice, or malpractice, of medicine. On the one occasion when he was confronted with this theory while under oath, Howe did not take the opportunity to refute it. Once, however, he gave another version of his life during the years when he might have been studying and practicing medicine. This was in an essay in self-praise published as the introduction to one of the advertising brochures the firm occasionally put out. "At the age of twenty," he wrote, "I entered King's College, London, with"—a wholly gratuitous bit of information but suggestive of a rather suspect eagerness to establish his whereabouts—"the son of that great American statesman and historian, Edward Everett, and succeeded in graduating with some distinction. Soon after, I entered the office of a Mr. George Waugh, a noted barrister. I had the good fortune to meet the commendation of Mr. Waugh, and I was consequently placed at the head of his corps of assistants, and frequently appeared in the London courts in place of my employer. My connection with this office lasted about eight years." He goes on to say that "in pursuance of an intention long prior formed" he returned to this country "in the early fifties." There would be no reason to question the truth of this story except for the fact that it raises some difficult questions of chronology. Howe was born in 1828. He says that he entered college at twenty, graduated, and worked eight years for Mr. Waugh. Assuming that he graduated from college the day after he entered it, and that Mr. Waugh employed him the day after that, he would still have been in England in 1856. The "early fifties" were already at least one year past, by anyone's definition. Moreover, what time does that leave for his prison sentence? Moreover and moreover, if Howe was really appearing in the London courts at the time he claims—in his own early twenties, that is—he was a barrister of rare precocity. In those days, as in these, men did not appear in the London courts except upon the completion of fairly long apprenticeships. There simply was not time enough for his own story to be true. Besides, if he did get here in the early fifties, something must be done about his more frequent stories that he got here in 1859. In his trial work, Howe was particularly admired for his skill in the handling of medical testimony.

The question of Howe's medical background came up in open court in 1874, when he and Hummel were being sued by a couple named William and Adelaide

Beaumont, who had retained Howe & Hummel to defend them against charges of white slavery and who maintained that they had in some fashion been cheated by the partners. The extant records of this case, which is, incidentally, just about the only known instance of a client expressing dissatisfaction with the services of Howe & Hummel, are in a few newspaper stories that stimulate curiosity but do not satisfy it. It is clear from the stories, though, that Howe's background was gone into at some length by the Beaumonts' attorney, Thomas Dunphy. Howe was asked by Dunphy to tell the jury why he had left England. Howe's lawyer, ex-Mayor A. Oakey Hall, objected on the ground that the question was immaterial. The objection was sustained. Howe was also asked if his license to practice medicine in England had been revoked. Hall again objected and was again sustained. The question may or may not have been material, but it seems unlikely that it would have been asked at all without some foundation for it, and if in fact it had been baseless, it should have caused Howe no embarrassment to say either that he had not lost his license or that, never having been a physician, he had no license to lose. Some other questions of interest were put to Howe at the Beaumont trial. He was asked if he was the same person as a William Frederick Howe wanted for murder in England. He said that he was not. He was asked if he was the same person as a William Frederick Howe con-

victed of forgery in Brooklyn a few years earlier. He
denied that he was that person. He did not, however,
deny that he had been a witness at a London murder
trial—a rather notable one, it would seem, for it is referred to simply as the Stansfield Case—in 1840 and at
another in 1844. In 1840 Howe was twelve. He was
sixteen in 1844. So far as the newspaper accounts show,
he was not asked to explain how it happened that,
twice before his beard had stiffened, he had been so
close to murder.

From 1860 on, the main lines of Howe's career became fairly plain, and his penchant for crime, whatever it amounted to, seems sublimated in his activity
in behalf of other criminals. Several reputable persons
first made his acquaintance in 1859, and it was generally his story that he had arrived here then. The
evolution from criminal into criminal lawyer was a
natural enough one in a period when, as Arthur Train
wrote, the criminal bar consisted mainly of unfrocked
priests, drunkards, ex-police magistrates, and political
riffraff of all sorts. "In those days," George W. Alger
has written, "there were practically no ethics at all in
criminal law and none too much in other branches of
the profession. The grievance committee of the bar
association was not functioning and a lawyer could
do pretty nearly anything he wanted. Most of them
did." At any rate, by 1861, Howe was practicing in

the local criminal courts, and in 1862 he seems to have put in a brief spell of military service. He is listed in Trow's City Directory for 1862 as Judge Advocate of the New York State Cavalry Brigade. There is no record of how or when he got his education in American law, but that in itself presents no mystery. The courts in those days were full of lawyers with no academic training—for some now obscure reason, men in this class were called "Poughkeepsie lawyers"—and a year or two in the office of any member of the bar would have sufficed. In 1863 the City Directory lists him as being again in private practice. It seems to have been around this time that he enjoyed his first real triumph as a pettifogger. The story was one he always enjoyed telling. A client of his had been convicted in the Court of Special Sessions, and Howe, in appealing the case, argued that justice had not been done the defendant because only two judges had sat throughout the entire case. Apparently one of the three judges who regularly sat in the court had excused himself briefly during the presentation of testimony in order to attend to some private business. Howe, to what he reported was the vast entertainment of his colleagues, made the temporary absence of one judge the basis of his appeal, arguing that his client had received only two-thirds of what the State Constitution describes as a fair trial. These lawyers told the inexperienced Howe that there were often times when only two judges heard an entire case and that no one had ever been foolish enough to challenge a conviction on that ground. In the General Term of the Supreme Court, however, the court agreed with Howe, the derision of the other lawyers turned to admiration, and a new legal star was born.

In the closing years of the Civil War, Howe became a widely sought-after lawyer. Having severed his own connections with the armed forces in 1863, probably early in the year, he was in the business of severing the connections of others. There are not many contemporary accounts of this phase of his work, but newspaper biographies of a few years later, around the time when he was becoming famous as a criminal advocate, report that during the war he was known as Habeas Corpus Howe because of his success in getting dispirited soldiers back into mufti on writs of habeas corpus. He would bring the reluctant warriors into court and have them depose· either that they had volunteered while drunk, which made their enlistments illegal and entitled them to discharge, or that, because of some circumstance in their family or business affairs, they had been conscripted contrary to law. Eugene Nadelman, an historian of the bar who has studied Howe's career, believes that Howe's success in these cases may have been the provocation for President Lincoln's unprecedented and still disputed suspension, by proclamation, of the right of habeas corpus throughout the entire country on September 15, 1863. (The right had previously been suspended only along certain military lines of communication.) His success could certainly have been a provocation to something. As usual, when he found a new device for frustrating justice, he put it to work on a mass-production basis. "During the war," according to a magazine article published in 1873, "Mr. Howe at one time secured the release of an entire company of soldiers, some seventy strong." According to Nadelman's researches, Howe was also engaged as counsel to large numbers of hoodlums indicted as a result of their participation in the New York draft riots of July 1863, which raged in an area of which his office was almost the exact center. The newspapers, however, have little to say of him in this period.

Howe emerges quite suddenly as the foremost criminal lawyer of his day. In the late sixties, he had been a person of some consequence around the Tombs, but his clientele had not been overly choice. It appears from the record to have consisted mainly of streetwalkers, pickpockets, and sundry misdemeanants. His pleading may have been more frequently successful than that of his competitors and his practice somewhat larger, but his reputation was something less than national. From the early seventies on, scarcely a prominent underworld figure shows up in a New York court without Lawyer Howe at his side, and the newspapers never refer to him without using some adjective or sobriquet suggestive of incomparability. Although it is difficult to find mention of him in the newspapers as late as 1869 and 1870, by January 25, 1873, it was possible for a magazine article about him, entitled "William F. Howe: The Celebrated Criminal Lawyer," to discuss him as an established institution: "Of the several justly noted gentlemen who have well-earned reputations before the bar of the metropolis of the Western Hemisphere, no single one, perhaps, contains so many elements of success as the subject of this sketch. Indeed, it has become almost a maxim that if any given case has a defense, he will be sure to find and use it; and a person charged with any crime may readily content himself with the conclusion that he will have, in him, the benefit of every possible circumstance that is available." The only event that accompanied this change from a modest local repute to almost universal acclaim was the establishment of the firm of Howe & Hummel in 1869, but, although the results of that joining of forces were to be notable in later years, it is doubtful if it helps much to explain Howe's sudden rise to eminence. Hummel had come to Howe as an office boy in 1863, when he was thirteen, and Howe soon spotted him as good legal timber. Hummel was not yet twenty when he was admitted to partnership with Howe, who was then forty-one. Hummel played an almost insignificant part in the firm's early cases. "While Lawyer Howe was making his eloquent address to the jury," the *Herald* reported in 1870, "he was assisted by his young and diminutive partner, Lawyer Hummel, who came running in and out of the courtroom with volumes of Shakespeare and Smollett, to which the defense counsel referred frequently for apt quotations." Hummel was a shrewd little lawyer even in those days, and he unquestionably brought more to the partnership than an ability to cart literature around. But the show in those days was all Howe's, and it was his genius at wheedling and coaxing juries that fetched the cash customers. From 1870 on, the big names begin appearing alongside his: Charles O. Brockway, the counterfeiter; Mother Mandelbaum; Western George; Peter De Lacey, the boss of the New York bookmakers; Hattie Adams and the French Madame, the procuresses; and all the rest.

The murderers signed up fastest of all. A survey made in the Tombs in January of 1873 showed that twenty-three of the twenty-five prisoners then awaiting trial for murder or manslaughter were Howe clients. Not all the 650 homicide defendants he counseled achieved newspaper celebrity, but he was on hand at nearly every celebrated trial in New York in his time. He snatched from the gallows such glamorous killers as Dr. Jakob Rosenzweig, known to crime fans as the Hackensack Mad Monster, a trunk murderer who was caught when he tried to express the dismembered body of a girl named—musically, as the papers pointed out—

Alice Augusta Bowlsby to Baltimore (three of Howe's clients dispatched bodies, or parts thereof, to Baltimore); Annie Walden, the Man-Killing Race-Track Girl; and Jack Hahn, the Castle Island Life Saver, a man whose preservative vocation seems oddly at variance with his casual way with a trigger. He was attorney to Carlyle Harris, a Columbia medical student whose morphine poisoning of his child-bride, Helen Potts Harris, is still being talked about by the older members of the older families in New York; to Michael McGloin, a leader of the Whyos, who, when discovered in the act of relieving a saloon till of its contents, murdered the barkeep, Louis Hanier, with a slingshot; to Danny Driscoll, one of McGloin's successors, who did in a Five Points debutante named Beezy Garrity; to Dr. Adolph Meyer, a physician who insured in his own favor the lives of his friends, then took them out in his rowboat on hot summer days and gave them cold beer cut with nitroglycerine, a beverage which, in the course of killing those it refreshes, produces symptoms superficially indistinguishable from ones caused by sunstroke; and to Martin Thorn, a Sixth Avenue barber who, with the help of his paramour, Augusta Nack, beheaded a man named Willie Guldensuppe and thereby gave William Randolph Hearst a story that helped him get started in the New York newspaper business. Howe's work on behalf of these homicidal clients was in addition to his labors in reducing an always overloaded calendar of cases involving such lesser crimes as mayhem, arson, burglary, assault, and all types and degrees of larceny.

Howe & Hummel unquestionably had a hand in many cases with which the firm was never officially or formally identified. Some histories of the underworld, for example, speak of Howe as the lawyer who put in the fix for Richard Croker, one of the great Tammany bosses, when Croker was charged with the murder, in 1874, of John McKenna, a car driver who had got mixed up in some rough stuff around a ballot box. Croker went on trial once, but the jury was unable to agree. Somebody's memory failed him, and Croker was never tried again. The exact maneuvers of the case, however, have been blacked out by Tammany's control of the records. It is only very recently that the truth of the firm's part in the Stokes-Fisk affair, which was the most famous murder case of the century next to Booth's killing of Abraham Lincoln, has been revealed. On January 6, 1872, Edward S. Stokes, a member of a wealthy Brooklyn family, shot Colonel James Fisk, Jr., speculator in stocks and gold, wrecker of the Erie Railroad, and the high priest of Gilded Age hedonism, on the staircase leading into the lobby of the Broadway Central Hotel. Fisk died of his wounds the following day. Stokes and Fisk had been rivals in business and in a recent libel suit, and they had both sought the affections of Josie Mansfield, a singularly beautiful young actress. Direct and circumstantial evidence of Stokes's guilt was abundant. But after three trials and a bewildering amount of legal finagling, Stokes got off with four years in the penitentiary. It was a scandalous miscarriage of justice, and cynics of the period had no difficulty in persuading others that money and prestige had bought Stokes his light penalty. It was said at the time, but never established, that Howe's notorious gift for lawyer's monkey business was also at Stokes's service, but it was never proved. Howe was not among the attorneys of record in the case, although John R. Dos Passos, the father of the contemporary novelist and a man who often took over for Howe & Hummel when it was felt that the name of the shyster firm would be a liability, was. When *Woodhull & Claflin's Weekly* published the survey of Tombs murder defendants that showed Howe representing twenty-three out of the total of twenty-five, it noted that Stokes was one of the two Howe did not represent. It added, however, that Howe had been "invited to assist in the defense of Stokes, but for reasons which cannot now be made public he declined." The statement is a peculiar one. If he was really not involved, what reason could he have for withholding anything?

The way in which the partners were involved in the Stokes-Fisk case was made clear three-quarters of a century after the murder in a letter published in *The New Yorker* for December 28, 1946, by Edgar Salinger, a

State Department employee who got it from Abe Hummel in Japan forty years ago. Mr. Salinger tells his own story rather engagingly:

I think it was in 1910 or thereabout that I happened one day to go to the Oriental Hotel in Yokohama and meet, in the lobby, a friend who, in turn, introduced me to a Mr. Hummel, who had just arrived in the city. During the conversation, it turned out that he was the famous Hummel of Howe & Hummel, the criminal lawyers, and as I was acquainted with the course of events, I realized that he had just finished serving his term in the penitentiary as a result of his conviction in New York City. This turned out to be the case.

Hummel made no bones about this and told us he was making a world tour to recuperate from his incarceration. He was an extremely affable little chap, a splendid raconteur, and we became very well acquainted. He stayed in Yokohama for some weeks and asked me to show him some of the sights in the native city and the notable points around Tokyo Bay, which I was very pleased to do. He spoke to me freely about his various activities, and I found him to have a very interesting personality.

One day we were walking along one of the streets, when a rickshaw passed by in which sat a man whom I shall identify as Dr. X for the reason that he though probably dead, has relatives living in this country. Dr. X had arrived in Japan many years previously. He lived very quietly. Nobody knew very much about him. He was married and had several daughters. He had never taken out papers entitling him to practice medicine in Japan. He did, however, hold a rather unimportant little position which paid him a small amount of money. It was in connection with the United States Consulate. He would go on board vessels clearing for American ports, and attend to the fumigation, after which he would issue health clearance papers permitting the vessel's departure from Japanese ports. The Doctor had one very noticeable peculiarity. He had an enormous, red, bulbous nose, something on the order of the famous nose of Mr. J. P. Morgan, Sr. This was the individual who was riding in the rickshaw past Hummel and myself.

As it went by, Hummel grabbed my arm and said, "My God, that was a ghost I never expected to see."

I said to him, "Why?"

"Well," he said, "you know this man?" I said, "Yes, He is Dr. So-and-so. He has lived here for a long time."

"Yes," said Hummel. "What else do you know about him?"

I said, "Nothing. Nobody around here knows much about him."

With that, he laughed and said, "Well, well, well—I'll tell you who he is. Did you ever hear of the famous murder case in which Stokes killed Jim Fisk in the Broadway Central Hotel in New York City?"

I said, "Yes. Of course, this was really before I was born, but as a New Yorker I know about the case."

"Well," said Hummel, "that was one of the most sensational murders ever perpetrated in New York City. Stokes shot Fisk in the lobby of the hotel as Fisk was coming down the stairway, but for one reason they never were able to get a first-degree murder conviction against Stokes. In court, there never was produced an actual eye-witness to the shooting. But, actually, there *had* been one man who saw the whole thing. That was the man who just passed on the street. He was in the lobby of the hotel and saw the whole shooting. We got to him quickly, paid him a huge amount of money to clear out of the country on the understanding that he would never put his foot back and would never let us know where he had gone. And so this is where he landed! The Doctor kept his bargain. That is why they were never able to hang Stokes!"

"But," said Hummel, "certainly strange things happen! I never thought that I would ever see this man on the streets of Japan as an indirect result of my having been in the penitentiary."

Endowing witnesses for life and sending them to Japan was a small part of Howe & Hummel's business. Mostly, their job was to win acquittals, and Howe, the principal acquittal-winner, won more often by the forceful pleading of conventional defenses than by the legal razzle-dazzle that has distinguished his best-known successors. Once, he set at liberty a professional arsonist named Owen Reilly by demonstrating to the court that it could not, unless it possessed superhuman wisdom, sentence Reilly to anything, even after Reilly had pleaded guilty to a felony. Reilly, one of a number of young men who supported themselves by setting fire to buildings for people who felt that the insurance on their properties was more to be desired than the uncertain revenues they might bring in the future, had ignited a row of stores on the lower East Side. He was arrested, and he retained Howe to defend him. Howe or some other legal eagle in the office read up on the statutes covering arson and found that by pleading Reilly guilty to attempted arson, rather than letting him stand trial for having committed arson, they could save the firm the bother of a trial and save Reilly the possible inconvenience of going to prison for the rest of his life. The District Attorney and the judge agreed to accept the lesser plea. When Reilly came up for sentence, Howe rose and solemnly stated that the law provided no penalty for the crime of attempted arson. The court begged enlightenment. The sentence for attempted arson, Howe said, like the sentence for any crime attempted but not actually committed, was half the maximum imposed by the law for the actual commission of the crime. The penalty for arson was life imprisonment, no less. Hence, if the court were to determine a sentence for Reilly, it would have to determine half a life. "Scripture tells us that we knoweth not the day nor the hour of our departure," Howe said. "Can this court sentence the prisoner at the bar to half of his natural life? Will it, then, sentence him to half a minute or to half the days of Methuselah?" The court agreed that the problem was beyond its earthbound wisdom. Reilly walked out, presumably to arm himself with a new supply of matches and tinder, and the legislature revised the arson statutes soon thereafter.

Once, in 1888, Howe very nearly forced the courts to declare an open season for murder. A cop-killer known as Handsome Harry Carlton had been convicted for the first-degree murder of Patrolman Joseph Brennan. He came up for sentence in December of 1888, the year the legislature abolished hanging as the established mode of execution and substituted electrocution. Howe studied the new edict, known as the Electrical Death Penalty Law, and discovered, to what must have been his ghoulish delight, that its authors had most seriously blundered. They had left an interval of almost seven months in which murder might be committed with impunity. The plan of the Legislature, when it had passed the law early in 1888, was to abolish hanging as of June 4 of that year and to institute electrocution on January 1, 1889; murderers convicted after June 4 were to be kept alive and in prison until the electric chair was ready. That was what it intended, but it was not what it said. The act provided that no one was to be hanged after June 4 and that electrocution was to begin on the first of the following year, but it carelessly went on to say that electrocution "shall apply to all convictions for crimes punishable by death on or after that date." Hence, the state had deprived itself of the legal power to execute anyone who killed with malice aforethought during a period of almost seven months. More than that, since death was the only punishment then provided for first-degree murder, no punishment at all could be prescribed. An act for which no penalty is prescribed by law cannot properly be called a crime. When Handsome Harry, standing at the bar, was asked by the court what he had to say about why judgment of death should not be passed against him, Howe stepped forward and told the court,

"He has this to say: He says that Your Honor cannot now pass any sentence of death upon him. He says that the Legislature by its enactment of Chapter 499 of the Laws of 1888, a statute passed, approved, and signed by the Governor . . ." The startled judge agreed that, by the wording of the law, he had no power to sentence Carlton or any other first-degree murderer. The newspapers made the most of the story, and the effect on the community was comparable to that of the Orson Welles' terror fifty years later, when a radio play about an imaginary invasion of the earth by men from another planet was widely mistaken for a news broadcast describing an actual event. The Tombs and every other place of detention in the state had not only the usual accumulation of murderers awaiting execution but also those who had been held over since June for the January unveiling of the hot seat. If Howe was upheld, all their sentences would be voided and the courts might be forced to dismiss all first-degree indictments for murders committed in the state between June 4 and December 31, 1888. Indeed, by extension, anyone who killed with intent in the remaining few weeks of the year could kill with impunity. The whole prospect was so distressing that Inspector Byrnes of the New York Detective Bureau and District Attorney Fellows had to release statements assuring the community that come what might, measures would be taken to insure its safety. They were not necessary. Howe was perfectly right in his reading of the law, but the higher courts took the position that no mere slip in syntax could be allowed to jeopardize human life and that the intent of the Legislature, no matter how awkwardly expressed, had not been to declare a Borgian holiday. Handsome Harry swung in the Tombs courtyard a few days after Christmas. He was the last man to hang there.

Howe saved more criminals by talking to juries than by finding flaws in the law, and his courtroom methods were frequently the subject of analysis in newspapers and at family breakfast tables. It was often said of him, as it has often been said of every good trial lawyer, that he was essentially an actor. The point was well enough taken but, as exposition, almost meaningless. It contains the same element of redundancy as, say, the statement that a particular writer is great because he is essentially a man of heightened sensitivity and is possessed of an uncommon aptitude with words. There have, of course, been great advocates who got along on the strength of learning or logic or some other minor attribute, just as there have been writers who were great in spite of tin ears and sluggish imaginations, but these have been the baffling exceptions, requiring much in the way of explanation and apology. Almost by defini-tion, as Dr. Johnson was once at pains to point out, a trial lawyer is an actor. The Anglo-Saxon criminal trial is theatrical in its basic structure, and the lawyer who cannot take advantage of its dramatic possibilities has approximately the same utility as a deaf fiddler or a blind rifleman. Howe was an actor all right, a superb one in a superbly hammy way, but his histrionic ability was his qualification for practice in the criminal courts, not his special distinction at the bar.

He not only played the assigned part of the advocate: he staged whole productions. Any lawyer worth his fee, for example, will wring tears and sympathy from a jury with talk about a defendant's grief-stricken mother, his faithful wife, and his innocent children. Howe did it, too, but the talk was only part of the act. He brought the wife and children right into the courtroom and sat them down on the front bench. He had them perfectly trained to enact cross-bar pantomimes of devotion and trust with the prisoner at the counsel table. If by chance a particular defendant did not have a pretty wife, fond children, or a snowy-haired mother, he was not for that reason deprived of the sympathy they might create on his behalf. Howe would supply them from the firm's large stable of professional spectators. Repulsive and apelike killers often turned up in court with lamblike children and wives of fragile beauty. There are several cases on record in which the bench felt called upon to rebuke Howe for insinuating to the jury that the incarceration or execution of a defendant who, to the best of the court's knowledge, was single and childless when he was arrested would bring tragedy into the lives of so many people seated about the courtroom; and there is one instance of a stern reprimand from a judge who felt that a jury was somehow being imposed upon when, just as Howe reached the family motif in his summation, a young lady on the front bench found it the appropriate moment to bare her breast to the infant in her arms and look tenderly in the direction of the prisoner at the bar.

According to one of the earlier accounts of Howe's career, he discovered the appeal to American juries of mothers and children when he was trying his first murder case in New York. The case, as reported, was quite a spectacular one. It took place in 1863, and the defendant was William Griffin, the first mate on a merchantman that had been commandeered by the Union. Griffin was a Confederate sympathizer and made several efforts to persuade the master of his ship to go South and run the blockade. The master refused. One day he was found dead in his cabin. Griffin asked the owners to make him master, but they declined to do so. A new captain was appointed. Griffin asked him to desert with the ship. He, too, refused, and he, too, died shortly thereafter. By the time the third master was found dead in his cabin, the suspicions of the owners and of the government authorities were aroused. The body of the third dead captain was sent to Boston, where the contents of the stomach were analyzed and

found to contain copper sulfide. Griffin was arrested
and retained Howe to defend him. There was no question as to his guilt; he offered to plead guilty to manslaughter, but the federal government, which was prosecuting the case, would not accept the plea because
of the element of treason in the crime. There were two
trials. In the first the jury disagreed because Howe had
made a strong case for the guilt of the government's
chief witness, the steward of the ship, who had testified that he had seen Griffin rubbing some substance
or other on the captain's claret glass. The government's
case in the second trial was the same, and Howe offered the same defense. This time, however, the United
States Attorney tried to influence the jurors by bringing in the three widows of the three murdered captains.
Howe saw the disadvantage at which this put him, but
he quickly overcame it. His own wife and his small
daughter were in court that day. He built his entire
summation around them. "Will you," he asked the jury,
"on the sole authority of this disreputable scullion
make that woman a widow—that child an orphan?" He
said the same thing in different language for over an
hour. Griffin was acquitted. "Probably there has never
occurred," one thoughtful reporter observed, "a better illustration than this of the ready adaptation of
circumstances to meet a sudden emergency."

When Howe spoke of mothers and children, he generally cried. He was an automatic weeper. He could

cry at will. "He was known as the most accomplished weeper of his day," Samuel Hopkins Adams wrote not long ago. "He could and would cry over any case, no matter how commonplace. His voice would quaver, his jowls would quiver, his great shoulders would shake, and presently authentic tears would well up in his bulbous eyes and dribble over. It was a sickening spectacle, but it often carried a jury to extraordinary conclusions." The dampness in the air must have been oppressive when Howe went to work. "After recess," the *Herald* said in an account of the trial of Annie Walden, the Man-Killing Race-Track Girl, who not long before had embroidered a gentleman's midriff with the contents of a six-shooter, "while Miss Walden, gently encouraged by her attorney, was telling her story in an almost inaudible voice, the third juror cried softly, the sobs of juror nine could have been heard in the corridors, and there was moisture in the eyes of all but one or two of the other jurors. The prisoner's many devoted friends held handkerchiefs to their eyes, and when Lawyer Howe spoke, his voice was full of tears." Miss Walden, too, was acquitted.

The lachrymose stage of a Howe trial was generally the closing one; the tears symbolized only one of several emotional experiences through which Howe led his auditors. He could make a jury laugh and he could frighten it into an acquittal. Once, he used sheer terror to free a killer. This was in the trial of Ella Nelson, another woman who had done in her sweetheart. Howe made his usual defense in such cases—that the man had been trying to commit suicide and that the woman, in wrestling the gun from him, had ended by doing, accidentally, what she had striven to prevent—and he saw that this time it was not going down so well. Francis L. Wellman, one of New York's most successful prosecutors, and a man who often opposed Howe, told the story several times in his books and in his lectures. "Howe," he wrote in one account, "simply frightened the jury into acquitting her. The summations had taken until far into the night, and the atmosphere in the courtroom was dark and eerie. Everyone was tired and nervous. The defendant, dressed all in black and wearing a heavy veil, sat facing the jury with her hands covering her face. Suddenly, as he came toward the end of his summation, Howe, still talking, walked over behind the prisoner and—his voice booming about what I do not know, for his words were obliterated in all our minds by what immediately followed—encircled her with his arms, took hold of each wrist, and flung them outward, at the same time grinding his fingernails into her flesh with a force that must have produced excruciating agony. Ella Nelson screamed as that jury and everyone else in the courtroom had never heard a human being scream before. Words can scarcely tell the effect it produced, but the records can. Howe ended his summation then and there. I was so nervous that I could scarcely muster my thoughts for my own address, and when I was done the jury, still unnerved, staggered from the courtroom, and came back with an acquittal in a few minutes. In the telling of it, there is nothing to suggest why the agonized wail of a defendant should secure her freedom; just as easily, one might suppose, it would signify her guilt. Nonetheless, Howe, the master of jurors, had calculated aright."

As an impresario, Howe did not ignore costume or make-up. He was himself one of the most eccentric and ornate dressers of the nineteenth century, and he was, like Carlyle and Weber & Heilbroner, a believer in the *mystique* of clothes. He co-ordinated his dress with the moods he wished to create. He kept a wardrobe of twenty or thirty suits in his office a half-block away from the Criminal Courts Building, and it was not unusual for him to get in and out of three or four outfits in a single day. If, for example, he was defending a prostitute, he would try to make his appearance subdued and fatherly; if, on the other hand, he was cross-examining drab fellows like Anthony Comstock or the Reverend Dr. Charles Henry Parkhurst, two reformers with whom he had a good many encounters, he would confront drabness with splendor. He maintained that the clothes he wore had their effect not only on the jury but on himself. He said that he could plead a cause better when his dress was in harmony with it. More likely than not, he had the press at least partly in mind when he sifted his wardrobe for the appropriate garments. It has been the experience of most advocates that dress has little effect on juries and that conspicuous clothing may indeed have the undesirable effect of making a jury less interested in a lawyer's plea than in his appearance. For Howe, though, it helped greatly with the newspapers. If a particular trial was dull copy, reader interest could always be created by describing the defense counsel's purple pants, his diamonds, and the sheer size of his wardrobe. The sartorial evolution of a Howe murder trial was from bejeweled elegance to chaste sombreness. He tried to make the opening days festive as possible, and he showed up wearing his full complement of diamonds and an ensemble featuring green, purple, or rose. He was at his gayest and most resplendent while picking a jury. Of the examination of talesmen he made short work. He would take almost anyone on his juries, and he would try as a rule to find the first twelve men acceptable. All he wanted of them was that they be of varying racial, religious, and occupational backgrounds. If the jury had at least one Catholic, one Protestant, one poor man, and one man of means, and representatives of one or two racial minorities, Howe was satisfied that it was fertile enough ground for the quick-growing seeds of dissension. Usually, the first dozen men would embody this ideal, and they would be flattered by Howe's unquestioning acceptance of their intelligence and integrity. After Howe and the jury had enjoyed the mutual pleasure of making one another's acquaintance, Howe and his clothes would become more business-like. Gradually, as the trial wore on and the case grew more and more serious in aspect, Howe cut himself down to only three or four diamonds, and the garish coats and checked trousers gave way to richly subdued blues and browns. On the final day of the trial, when his client's fate hung in the balance and Howe was faced with the serious business of extracting tears from the jury, he would appear in a dark gray sack suit, adorned with not so much as a single diamond to brighten the grim proceedings.

Howe maintained an interest in his homicide defendants long after the lawyer-client relationship was over. He was like a good schoolmaster who likes to follow the careers and glory in the achievements of his old boys for years after they have left his tutelage. There is, in the possession of a relative of one of his associates, a folder of the correspondence he carried on with several murderers following their acquittals. It is curious stuff indeed, full of talk about fate and judgment and the hereafter, but the owner of the collection will not permit it to be quoted. In the cases of clients who were hanged, Howe continued the association as long as circumstances permitted. He attended the hangings. He would always be among the first on hand for the early-morning executions in the Tombs courtyard. He dressed for these events as for a funeral. He used to say that he attended hangings because the sound of a snapping spine and the sight of a body swinging from the rope fired him with the resolution to see to it, so far as he was able, that the gallows would claim no more victims. This was either self-deception or pure humbug. The truth was that he often put as much zest into helping to send a non-client to the gallows as he did in securing the acquittal of clients. When he was not preparing speeches to save his own clients from death, he would amuse himself by helping his friends in the District Attorney's office to convict other lawyers' clients. He once did this in the case of a murderer whom he later had to defend. The murderer was young Carlyle Harris, the wife-poisoner.

"Will you pardon me for suggesting," Howe wrote to Francis Wellman, who was prosecuting Harris in the original trial, "that in the Harris case, in the course of your speech, you say to the jury, 'Accompany me to the grave of this poor poisoned girl.' Then turn to her husband (the prisoner) and say to him, 'You dare not go to that spot. You put her there, she whom you swore to love, cherish, and protect, and you would hear through the sod which covers her remains the cry of "Murderer! Murderer!" Over that grave, to which this poor girl was prematurely sent by the hand of this assassin, write your verdict—'tis that of Guilty. From the grave the cry comes forth that this verdict must be rendered,' etc. You will excuse, I know, this suggestion. You may use it after your own fashion, and I think that if you look pointedly in the eyes of the accused when you dare him to accompany you to the grave of his victim, he will flinch and that you will make a strong point to the jury."

Wellman took Howe's advice and used almost exactly the words Howe had prepared for him. The speech was generally accounted a fine one, and Harris did flinch. He was speedily convicted. Dissatisfied with his counsel's handling of the case, he employed Howe. Howe and Harris became fast friends for the remainder of Harris' brief life. The two stood together at the bar when word came down from the Court of Appeals that Harris' conviction and the sentence of death had been upheld. In what must have been a carefully rehearsed scene, Howe, upon hearing the decision, took a flask of whisky from his pocket and offered Harris a drink. At the same moment, Harris produced an envelope and handed it to Howe. "I want you to have these, Mr. Howe," Harris said. "They are diamond cuff links. They are the last present Helen ever gave me. I am sure she would want you to have them." Howe sported the cuff links the rest of his life and said they were his favorite jewels. "My feelings for that noble and much persecuted youth could not have been deeper had he been my own son," Howe often said.

When Howe was working for acquittals, the day of summation was the big one. He relied more on his closing speech to the jury than on any other phase of his work. He was a competent coaxer and browbeater of juries but not a great one. Francis Wellman's *Art of Cross-Examination*, the definitive work on trial procedure, gives Howe credit for only one innovation in the questioning of witnesses. This is what Wellman calls the "silent examination." It applies principally to expert witnesses, doctors and the like, and it consists of leaving to opposing counsel the job of testing the credibility of one's own witnesses. The theory is that a jury is more impressed if a witness establishes his authority in the hostile atmosphere of cross-examination than if he does so at the urging of the counsel who employed him. The contribution is distinctly a minor one, and Howe never made much of it. The summation was the thing, and he was the most effective jury orator of his day. It is difficult now, however, to grasp exactly what it was in his speeches that made juries rise so often to his bait. Not even humor is as perishable as courtroom oratory, and Howe's oratory, read now, seems absurd and spongy. The letter to Wellman is a fair enough sample. The style was a caricature Victorian. It was prolix, ornate, and sonorous.

His sentences were long and rhythmical, but the rhythms, in print at any rate, are more soporific than stirring. He was master of the lawyer's tautology, the battered ornament, and the cliché. Almost without exception his clients were "more sinned against than sinning." When they were poor (nearly all Howe clients were poor, despite their ability to pay him large fees; poverty with Howe was not a matter of income but of the tatters he could find to dress his clients in) they were "wretched souls passed over in this world of tears by fortune and by providence alike." Toward the end of almost every summation, Howe would challenge the mercy of the jurors by throwing his impoverished clients at them with:

> *Over the stones rattle his bones*
> *He's only a pauper whom nobody owns.*

Yet the stuff went down. Probably its effectiveness was less a matter of language than of passion. He had a voice as powerful as a Roman general's, and he could work himself up into the most frightful lathers. "Mr. Howe here," said the *Herald* in 1888 describing his summation in defense of a murderer, Burton Webster, "by a series of what may be termed facial gymnastics portrayed every emotion known to human nature, including many phases that never, perhaps, were before known, or even thought of, and Mr. Howe's voice ranged from pianissimo to fortissimo and from deep bass to as near falsetto as he could get without danger to his vocal apparatus." There was nothing he would not do to get his effects. Once he made an entire summation, hours long, on his knees. He could make a jury believe anything. In the Ella Nelson case, pleading accident, he made the jury believe that Miss Nelson's trigger finger had accidentally slipped not once but six times. Perhaps his most spectacular piece of speechmaking was his defense of a man named Edward Unger, who after killing his lodger, a certain Bolles, had thrown Bolles' head into a ferryboat paddle wheel and had, like the Hackensack Mad Monster, sent the rest of the body to Baltimore, that inexplicably popular boneyard. The prosecution based its theory of premeditation on the care with which Unger had disposed of his client's remains. Howe made no attempt to refute this entirely reasonable contention until the very end of his speech. Then, as though seized by a vision, he announced to the jury that Unger had killed Bolles in an uncontrollable fit of passion and had cut him up as a humane and fatherly afterthought. In fact, he said, Unger had not really dismembered Bolles at all. The hand had been his, but the force that guided the hand was the three- or four-year-old daughter, apparently genuine, whom Unger was at that moment dandling on his knee. As Howe developed this story, Unger had had to get rid of Bolles' body in order to spare his child the sight of death. "Yea," Howe said, " 'twas she who really did it, 'twas she, 'twas she. This innocent child, this lamb of God, guided the hand of this miserable wretch into his horrible deed. He knew, yes, even this lowly creature, knew that he could never face his Maker after curdling the soul of this babe with the sight of what her father had done. Could you send a man to his death for what a child hath done, for what a man hath done for the love of child?" The jury could not. Unger got off with manslaughter.

Howe was a pioneer of the insanity defense in this country. Whenever the facts of a killing could not be tailored to fit a theory of accident, suicide, or self-defense, he pleaded insanity or the then related defense of epilepsy. It has been stated by one authority on the subject that Howe was the first man to get the courts to recognize delusions as prima facie evidence of insanity, rather than the products of vain and evil minds. He is also credited with being the first man to establish in law, thirty years before the Thaw case, the theory of "impulsive" or temporary insanity. Indeed, it is possible that Howe, and not, as is commonly supposed Delphin Delmas, Thaw's lawyer, coined the word "brainstorm" to describe a sudden fit of insane criminality. For the most part, though, Howe's insanity defenses were on a low psychiatric level. In one case, he based a successful insanity defense on the peculiar shape of his client's head. The man, whose picture can still be studied in a self-advertising pamphlet pub-

lished by Howe & Hummel, was indisputably an odd
specimen of human architecture, but he was nevertheless the author of a murder that showed a certain ability
to reason and plan. Nevertheless, Howe insisted that
he was a lunatic. "Look at that unsymmetrically formed
cranium," he told the jury, pointing toward the defendant's skull. "Observe the wild, the vacant, the
idiotic, the imbecilic appearance. I tell you, he is
NATURE'S MADMAN." (The capitals appear in
the court records and probably indicate shouting.)

Wellman, in one of his books, recalled a Howe client
who came into court with his head swathed in yards
of white muslin, as if to suggest an ailment of the mind
that required bandaging lest the brains fall out or at-
tract infection. Wellman, as prosecutor, told the jury
that he had questioned the defendant before the trial
and that the man's head had then been unbandaged
and apparently unlacerated. But it did no good.
Throughout the whole trial the prisoner simulated a
kind of village idiot's tic, "twitching the right corner
of the mouth," Wellman said, "and simultaneously
blinking the left eye." As soon as this idiot left the
court, however, "the defendant's face resumed its
normal composure, except for the large grin that
covered it as he lightly removed the cloths from about
his forehead." Apparently, Howe used bandages on
several occasions, for there is a report of a case in 1873
in which the defendant, one William Blakely, came

into court with his head tied up, and, when he heard the jury's verdict of not guilty, "leaped from his seat, gave one loud shout of joy, tore the now useless bandage from his head, and speedily disappeared." Wellman told a story of a prisoner whose insanity, according to Howe, was accompanied by muteness, and who, having testified in an improvised sign language, walked over to his lawyer at the happy conclusion of the trial and said, "Silence is golden." The story is too good not to be apocryphal, but it suggests the measure of Howe's inventiveness.

Another notable acquittal through simulated lunacy was in the case of Alphonse Stephani, a wealthy young man who had murdered his late father's attorney, one Clinton G. Reynolds, because the attorney was not settling the estate to Stephani's satisfaction. Unlike the killer with the irregular head, Stephani tended to be rather attractive in his general contours. A graphic description of what Howe's make-up did for him survives in the address to the jury by the Assistant District Attorney who was trying the case. "Instead of the handsome, neatly dressed rich man's son whom we saw before this trial opened," the prosecutor told the jury, "you jurors saw a wild, unkempt creature, a Caliban in ugliness. Stephani's hair, let me tell you, had been untouched by shears or brush for months. He still wears the clothes he had on when arrested, but the fine linen is now in tatters and almost black. His outer garments are greasy and crusted with accumulations of intentionally spilled food. Not a word has he spoken to anyone, he whose speech was once so fine and elegant. With large black eyes as deep and mournful as Edwin Booth's, he has stared gloomily at nothing. Lear was a model of sanity beside him. But now let us look at the facts. There has been some testimony to show that he had fallen off a horse many years ago. . . ." But the prosecutor's facts made poor evidence compared with what the jurors saw. Stephani was not convicted.

Curiously, there are no recorded instances of Howe fixing or even attempting to fix, a juryman. He and Hummel had bribed judges, suborned perjury, and engaged in every other malpractice, but the record is clean on juries. Yet in spite of the record, and in spite of the low esteem in which virtue generally was held in the Howe & Hummel office, there was never so much as a single charge of jury-fixing on Howe's part. More likely than not the record is clean because the attempts that were made were successful. Even the most forceful advocates, for example Bill Fallon, have at some time or another deemed it wise to insure themselves against the day when their powers of persuasion may weaken. On the other hand, it is doubtful if very many of Howe's jurors were ever reached by anything but his speeches. He was enormously proud of his ability to make a jury do his bidding by the turn of a soggy phrase or by a bit of Smithfield mummery, and he would probably have considered it unsporting to have too many of his acquittals arranged for in advance. In fact, the vast contempt for jurors bred in him by his manipulation of them was once made the cause of his undoing by the late Judge Horace Russell, who, as a young prosecutor, was one of the few men to discover a way of beating Howe in a jury trial. "Gentlemen of the Jury," Russell once said at the close of a trial, "I am shocked to see that you were not indignant over the sickening flattery that has come from the lips of Mr. Howe. Now I do not, as he pretends to do, consider you the brainiest and handsomest men in the world, but merely as belonging to the ordinary run of mortals. But I can see from your self-satisfied faces that there will be a miscarriage of justice by the acquittal of this prisoner. You know, I really ought not to have been assigned to prosecute the prisoner, being such a tyro at the bar. So there is little I can say by way of argument to induce you to do your duty, which you are now about to shirk. But I must tell you this sequel: after the scandalous acquittal which will follow your deliberations in the jury room, I should like you to know that I shall have a visitation from this man Howe. He will be once again arrayed in the diamonds he wore here on the first day of the trial, and there will be a wide grin substituted for the tears you have seen. There will be nothing lachrymose about him as he plants himself in a comfortable chair in my office and, with his feet up on my desk, delivers himself of this estimate of you: 'Horace, what perfect damned fools these jurors are.'" Howe lost the case.

CHAPTER THREE

LIGHT OF THE
TENDERLOIN

SOMETIME in the eighties, Howe & Hummel began broadening its practice to include such civil matters as divorce, breach of promise, and theatrical contracts and copyright. By 1890, the firm enjoyed, in addition to its near monopoly over the legal business of organized crime, the patronage of almost the entire theatrical community, a divorce practice larger than that of any other firm in the city, and a breach-of-promise blackmail racket that was said to have enriched the partners by well over a million dollars in the course of its operations. There is nothing in the surviving records to explain why the firm entered these new fields when it did, but it is possible that

Howe and Hummel, who were as farsighted as they were crooked, decided to branch out because they foresaw a depression in organized crime. The fifteen or twenty years after their firm was established were good ones for crime and criminals in New York, as they were, in fact, for almost everyone in New York. Pickpockets and safe-crackers were assured of finding well-stuffed pockets and safes, and political protection was cheap and generally reliable. The destruction of the Tweed Ring in 1871 made little difference. The Flash Age went right on. The reformers who took over the city then were even less effectual than most reformers, and Honest John Kelly, who became the next boss of Tammany, was as corrupt as Tweed if not as daring. There was no real reform until the mideighties, and it was around this time that Howe & Hummel began to build up a civil practice.

By the middle eighties, quite a bit of life had come into the District Attorney's office. Howe & Hummel profited momentarily, since more prosecutions meant more defenses, but in the long run the effects were not good. The District Attorney gathered in seventy-four madams in one raid—Howe & Hummel represented the whole job lot of them—and organized vice was on its uppers for several years thereafter. The law was closing in on George Leonidas Leslie, alias Western George, when George, almost decomposed, was found on Tramp's Rock in the Bronx, dead either by his own hand or by that of an ambitious lieutenant. George, a bank robber less romantic than Jesse James but more successful in a business way, was given a decent burial by Mother Mandelbaum, the East Side shopkeeper who was the matriarch of the New York underworld as well as its most successful receiver, but the ceremonies were barely over when Mother Mandelbaum had to catch a train for Canada, where she lived for the rest of her life. The D.A.'s office, by hiring whole platoons of Pinkerton detectives to do the job which the kept police refused to do, had at last managed to have her indicted, and she and her attorneys, Howe & Hummel, thought conviction so likely that she jumped bail. The death of Leslie and the expatriation of Mother Mandelbaum deprived Howe & Hummel of two of their best clients. Between them, they had probably contributed half a million dollars or more to the firm's income over the years.

In 1885, De Lancey Nicoll, an able lawyer and an eloquent spokesman for the upright life, joined the D.A.'s staff and embarked upon a succession of notable prosecutions. Howe & Hummel clients were picked off in alarming numbers in spite of the lawyers' most ingenious and forceful defenses. A few years later, the Reverend Dr. Charles Henry Parkhurst, of the Madison Square Presbyterian Church, began to tell what he knew about the protection given to prostitutes, gamblers, and criminals by the city's politicians and police.

As a result of Dr. Parkhurst's work, the governor of
the state set up the Lexow Committee, whose investiga-
tions were as devastating to Tammany Hall—and thus
to organized crime—as the later work of Samuel Sea-
bury and Thomas E. Dewey. Then came Mayor
William Strong and his reform administration, whose
most active member was its excitable young Police
Commissioner, Theodore Roosevelt, and then another
state investigation, by a group known as the Mazet
Committee. Throughout these politically hygienic
years, Howe & Hummel had a busy enough time defending all the wrongdoers who were being indicted,
but with so many of their steady customers going to
jail, there was good reason to give some thought to
the possibilities in civil practice.

It was, ironically, in part the fault of Howe & Hummel that the Lexow investigation, which started so
much of the trouble, was ever made. It never would
have been made but for the work of Dr. Parkhurst,
and his work would have come to nothing had it not
been for a spectacular legal bull on the part of Howe
& Hummel. For several months, Dr. Parkhurst, who
had been called to his pastorate in Gomorrah from a
church in Lenox, Massachusetts, had been denouncing
the city government for countenancing the crime and
vice he saw, or thought he saw, all about him. His
sermons, every one of them a gem of homilectic ele-

gance, were much admired by his parishioners, but they got little attention from anyone else, and nothing came of them until one Sunday in 1892 a newspaperman, probably having lost his way somewhere else, happened to attend the church. Struck by the vigor of the minister's attacks, he wrote an article for his paper, quoting Dr. Parkhurst's description of the city officials as "the polluted harpies that, under the pretense of governing this city, are feeding day and night on its quivering vitals . . . a lying, perjured, rum-soaked, libidinous lot." The results were most encouraging. Prose like that was not to be had in just any neighborhood church. Not only churchgoers but the newspapers began to discuss the merits of the minister's accusations. In these discussions, it was occasionally pointed out that while Dr. Parkhurst's sermons were forceful in their language, they were occasionally weak in their factual content. To remedy this defect, Dr. Parkhurst, later that year, made what quickly and justly became the most celebrated tour of the underworld in New York's history. He went on this expedition in the company of a reformed criminal, an honest lawyer, and a parishioner named John Langdon Erving, a young man in whom virtue shone so brightly that he was known to his friends and his pastor as Sunbeam Erving. The ex-criminal led his three companions, who wore turtle-neck sweaters and checked caps in order to look like toughies on a spree, into the most rancidly sinful dives he knew of. Returned from this tour of hell, Dr. Parkhurst began a new series of sermons. He said that he would not soil his pulpit by describing the degradation he had seen, but he did characterize it, and he announced that he would give the details to the District Attorney, behind closed doors, if the District Attorney cared to listen. The District Attorney did not care to listen; at least, he did not share the bloodhound's usual eagerness to take up the scent. Dr. Parkhurst went right on. Intimating that the Borgias would have blushed and Nero stopped his fiddling had they seen what he had seen, he continued to throw down his challenges Sunday after Sunday. Finally, in deference to the section of public opinion which held that Dr. Parkhurst's charges should at least be looked into, the District Attorney had his detectives raid the Twenty-seventh Street brothel of Hattie Adams, the place in which, Dr. Parkhurst had said, he had seen the most unspeakable iniquities of all.

Ordinarily, the raid and the arrests that followed it would have been only a gesture, an inexpensive one at that. Hattie Adams had been arrested before, and it was the custom of her lawyers, Howe & Hummel, to plead her not guilty in magistrate's court, then change the plea to guilty when the case came to trial in the Court of General Sessions. It was the custom of the General Sessions judges to fine her twenty-five or fifty dollars and set her free. This time, according to Terence McManus, the foremost living authority on the history of the New York criminal bar, who was in the District Attorney's office in the early nineties, Inspector Thomas F. Byrnes of the Detective Bureau, the author of the definitive *Byrnes' Professional Criminals of the United States*, had a bright idea which he thought would not only save Hattie the slight expense of the fine but would silence Dr. Parkhurst for good. He explained it to Howe & Hummel, and they liked it. Byrnes's idea was to plead Hattie *not* guilty in General Sessions and have her stand trial. Byrnes had reasoned, and Hattie's lawyers had agreed, that if they put Hattie on trial, Dr. Parkhurst could prove her guilt only by telling the court and the newspapers the things he wished to tell only to the District Attorney in private. Hattie had been arrested on his complaint, and it would therefore be up to him to give the testimony that would convict her. "They figured," McManus says, "that sooner than do that he would head back to Massachusetts, which was just where they wanted him to head."

They figured wrong, though. Howe & Hummel had had a good deal of experience in court with the other eminent sin-hater of the day, Anthony Comstock, and had outwitted him every time. But Dr. Parkhurst was neither the fool nor the craven Comstock was. He was, at this stage, receiving expert guidance from Jacob Riis and from Lincoln Steffens, who once called the old gentleman the precursor of the whole muckraking movement. Compelled to put up or shut up, Dr. Parkhurst put up. Hattie stood trial, and when Dr. Parkhurst was called upon to testify, he braced himself manfully and walked to the witness stand. "Would that this chalice should be taken from my lips," he was overheard whispering to Sunbeam Erving as he rose from his seat. When the District Attorney had finished with Dr. Parkhurst, Howe & Hummel each had a go at him on cross-examination, and so did one of their assistant Torquemadas. They said that he was a clerical voluptuary whose crusade against vice and sin gave him a chance to enjoy it. "In the words of M. Thiers," Howe said to the court, "I cannot elevate him to the level of my contempt. Speak as you will of her, Hattie Adams is worth a thousand of his kind." "They are truly the devil's advocates," Dr. Parkhurst later told the press. "But they never unsettled me." He had not been unsettled even by the three attractive young ladies brought to court by Howe & Hummel and instructed to sit up front and unsettle him by fastening their eyes upon him throughout his testimony. They listened with a simulation of brazen curiosity while Dr. Parkhurst went into the details of the evening he had spent *chez* Hattie, and they alternately giggled and looked shocked when he had purposefully gone out of his way in search of material. Still, he went resolutely on. He told of a midnight "circus" he had seen and about a game of leapfrog he had played with nude prostitutes, in order, he said, to persuade them that he really was a "sport from Chicago." He was followed to the stand by Sunbeam, who corroborated his testimony. Later, Dr. Parkhurst told what he had learned about the police protection Hattie Adams was receiving, and he introduced documents of unassailable authenticity showing that protection could be had at a price by anyone in the vice business in New York. That did it. The Legislature, dominated as usual by upstate Republicans, set up the Lexow Committee, and Tammany Hall and its Police Department were taken to the cleaners once again. Howe & Hummel defended several of the politicians and dozens of the cops who were indicted, but when it was all over, a lot more of their clients and friends were in jail or unemployed. Even Inspector Byrnes, whose bright idea it was to let Hattie stand trial, found that he had been too bright for his own good. He was demoted by the next administration and eventually dropped from the force.

It may have been the hard times upon which organized crime was falling that sent Howe & Hummel venturing into new fields of enterprise, or it may have been the ambitions of Abe Hummel. Hummel, who had been only nineteen when he became Howe's partner in 1869, was reaching his prime in the eighties, and his talents and tastes were all for civil practice.

The tradition of shystering he represented was very different from Howe's. Howe was an old-style criminal lawyer who specialized in the classic crimes of violence and larceny. The courtroom was his workshop, and it was his knowledge of courtroom tricks and his willingness to use any of them, from crocodile tears to judge-fixing, that so consistently cheated the jailers and hangmen. Howe knew the criminal law thoroughly—he collaborated with District Attorney Daniel Rollins on a codification of New York penal law that was widely in use until fifteen or twenty years ago—but he was gifted not so much with intellect as with voice, personality, and dramatic instinct. He had the voice of a pre-Stanislavsky tragedian and the personality of an accomplished carnival grifter. Whether or not it was true that he had been, at some time in his uncertain and mysterious youth, a professional remittance man of some sort, it would certainly not be inexact to describe the acquittals he cozened from jurors as the ill-gotten gains of a superbly played con game. Hummel was plainly cast from another die. He was, for one thing, all mind. He lacked Howe's sense of theatre and his expansive, gasconading manner, but he had, as Howe did not have, a brain of speed and precision. Even physically, he seemed to be mostly gray matter. Caricaturists drew him as a Humpty Dumpty with an egg head and a body of split toothpicks. There were a good many rather amiable sides to Hummel's character, but they were not of the sort to bring out the sympathy and good will of jurors. Jurors are always suspicious of a lawyer who looks smart, and Hummel could not, as Howe could, flatter a jury into sycophancy or hammer it senseless with talk. But he was Howe's superior in hair splitting, loophole finding, logic chopping, and all the other black arts which have made revolutionaries, ever since Jack Cade and Dick the Butcher, think about killing all the lawyers, first thing. There was in him something of Vholes, Buzfuz, Solon Shingle, and all the other archetypal lawyers of literature.

Hummel was born in Boston in 1849 or 1850, of German-Jewish parents who had probably come to this country in the 1848 wave of emigration from Germany. He was two or three when his parents moved to New York. He was brought up in the section near what is now Tompkins Square but what was then the center of the German-Jewish colony. The family was always poor. Hummel's father made his living, such as it may have been, selling playing cards to *stuss* players in East Side saloons. Hummel once told William O. Inglis that he earned his first dollar one summer day during the Civil War by going out with a pailful of tap water and a dipper to Tompkins Square, where a regiment of Union volunteers was massed under an oppressive sun and hawking "cold, clear water, fresh from Croton," to the soldiers. In 1863, right after receiving his diploma from Public School Number Fifteen, he began looking for a job. He found one as an office boy for Howe, who, having recently risen to an eminence somewhat above the run of Tombs shysters, had just converted the ground floor of the Centre Street store building into a law office that could take business right in off the sidewalk. Hummel's duties at first were mainly custodial. He washed the windows and he swept the floors. There were no big doors whose handles needed polishing, but there were plenty of papers—probably, at that time, fake habeas corpuses for the most part— to be copied in a big round hand. There was also his employer's stock of liquor and cigars to be replenished every few days, and there was coal to be carted from the safe where the coal scuttle was kept to the stove that stood in the waiting room. He could not have worked at these chores very long before Howe saw in him the makings of a lawyer and set him to reading case reports. Howe seems to have been genuinely fond of Hummel, to have been proud rather than resentful of Hummel's superior mental resourcefulness, and to have regarded his quick, foxy mind as the perfect accompaniment of his own special genius. "You'll have to see my little Abie about that," he would say whenever he was confronted with a problem requiring delicate ratiocination. "He's so smart." Hummel, according to one of his own accounts, actually began to practice in 1867, when he was seventeen and Howe was thirty-nine. A little more than a year later, the partnership was formed, and the Howe & Hummel shingle, all forty feet of it, was hung.

Under Howe's guidance, Hummel became a first-class criminal lawyer and a competent trial man. In the early days of the partnership, he assisted Howe in homicide defenses and even pleaded a few of his own. But trial work was not what he liked most, and, as time went on, he and Howe evolved a division of labor and responsibility that satisfied both men and made it possible for them to handle anything the underworld had to offer. Howe handled the trials. All the murderers, bank robbers, and brothel keepers were his charges. Hummel took on the more complex criminal matters, such as gambling, fraud, and prize-fighting, which was then illegal. While Howe was down the block dazzling jurors with his diamonds and fouling their thought processes with his sonorous oratory, Little Abe holed up in his office and put his brains at the service of bookmakers, bucket-shop proprietors, and all the fancier elements of the firm's criminal clientele. He represented the Poolsellers Association, a combine formed by bookmakers and policy-shop owners to defend their interests against Anthony Comstock's crusades; Hungry Joe and Kid Miller, two celebrated card sharps; Steve Brodie and a number of other owners of local dives; and Richard Kyle Fox, the leading fight promoter of the day as well as the editor and publisher of the *Police Gazette*. During the eighties and nineties, Hummel worked out the defense that became standard in nearly all the prize-fighting cases the firm handled—that the fight had been a scientific exhibition of boxing skill and that the participants had no intention of hurting each other—and he is generally accorded a good deal of the credit for eventually getting the sport legalized in New York State. As Anthony Comstock lobbied through the Legislature law after law designed to put the bookmakers and policy shops out of business, Hummel followed in his wake, testing the legality of each new act and finding ways through and around each new legal barrier the courts had upheld. "That firm had a perfect setup," one lawyer who recalls Howe & Hummel said recently. "You might say that Hummel was the man you saw when you wanted to commit a crime without getting caught. He could tell you if the ice was thick enough to hold you up. If you went ahead on his advice and got into trouble anyway, or if you got over where the ice was too thin, Howe was there to get you out. He would see that nothing very serious happened if you did get caught."

It was often said that it was Hummel who worked up most of the queer and clever defenses offered by Howe at jury trials. "In all their cases," as Arthur Train put it, "the voice was the voice of Howe, but the hand was the hand of Hummel." This could only have been

partly true, for Howe had wrought a substantial number of miracles before he ever met Hummel. Nevertheless, Hummel's trickiness was sometimes useful in
Howe's department. In the trial of Mrs. Ann E. Burns,
on a charge of manslaughter, Howe's most fervent
pleading proved, for some reason or other, unavailing.
The jury convicted her without even leaving the jury
box. Hummel, who often argued appeals in the superior
courts, where there were no juries to impress, took
over the case and got a reversal, on the ground that
Mrs. Burns had been convicted in a nonexistent court.
Her trial had been on the calendar for the November
term of General Sessions. The calendar was a long one,
and Mrs. Burns's trial ran over into December. The
judge forgot, at the start of the new month, to an-
nounce the adjournment of the November term and
the convening of the December term. Mrs. Burns was
convicted by the sitting jurors on December 7th. Hummel argued that it was a mockery of justice to permit
a December conviction in a November term. The
higher courts upheld him, and Mrs. Burns went free.

Hummel's methods as a divorce lawyer and his work
as a blackmailer were an open secret through all the
years he carried on. They were the subject of jokes
in the newspapers and on the stage. "What's that?"
a straight man would ask a vaudeville comic when a
noise like thunder sounded from the wings. "Why,

that's Howe & Hummel filing an affidavit," the comic said. The gag was not obscure, at least to the kind of people who could afford musical comedies. Howe & Hummel affidavits were as much a hazard of philandering as the house detective. Generally, they charged seduction under the promise of marriage, and they were redeemable by the alleged seducers at sums varying between five and ten thousand dollars, cash, half of which went to the disappointed young ladies and half to Howe & Hummel. Lawyers still alive who represented the victims of this blackmail estimate that the number of men shaken down by Hummel between 1885 and 1905 must have been well up in the hundreds. It is a curious fact, though, that while everyone knew what Hummel was up to and everyone knew of a victim or two, the total number of Hummel's victims and the identity of all but a handful has never been known or recorded.

Very few persons ever complained of getting less than they paid for from Howe & Hummel, and those who paid for concealment got it. When the firm laid a ghost, it stayed laid. A few names, however, did get into the public domain either as a result of subsequent litigation or through the uncontrollable leakage of gossip, and those whose involvement did become a matter of almost public record make up quite a representative list of seducers. They include a United States Senator of enduring reputation, the owner of one of the city's largest department stores, the heir to a still extant fortune based on another department store, the eldest son of a great railroad consolidator, a man who made a fortune developing uptown real estate, and the heir to several million dollars made in Coney Island concessions. Beyond these, however, not many became known to the public. Lawyers who represented some of the victims know, of course, who they were, but professional confidences restrain them from telling. "I wish I could talk about those I knew," a retired member of Dos Passos Brothers said recently, "but I can't do it. But there's nothing to stop me from saying that I must have represented more than a dozen of them myself, and I was only one of several lawyers in my own circle of acquaintances who had to go around and see Little Abe every so often. I'd say that, all told, there were more than five hundred who had to shell out at one time or another, and it wouldn't jar me a bit to hear that it hit a thousand. And you want to bear in mind that most of them were well-known and re-spected people—big merchants, politicians, members of old families, and all that. And a few bishops, too, I've heard. New York has never seen anything like it."

Hummel was the most systematic of blackmailers. He did not sit idly by waiting for soiled doves to fly in his office window. He was constantly beating the bushes for fresh affidavit copy. He assigned two of his employees, Lewis Allan and Abraham Kaffenburgh, who was his nephew, to go out along Broadway and the Bowery in search of unexploited seductions. Allan and Kaffenburgh became as familiar figures backstage as scene shifters and wardrobe mistresses. They would make the acquaintance of young actresses and chorus girls and explain to them how, by friendly co-opera- tion with Howe & Hummel, last year's infatuations could be converted into next year's fur coats. They had the girls rummaging around in their memories for old seductions the way antique dealers get home owners tearing up their attics in search of old glassware and ladderback chairs. When a girl came across with a likely story, she was escorted downtown to Hummel, who got the details from her and set them down in affidavit form. The existence of the affidavit would then be made known to the man named in it, and he was given his choice of breach-of-promise suit with wide publicity and with no details spared or a quick settlement. It was often charged that these affidavits were faked from start to finish and that Hummel was also the manager of a kind of badger game, in which his young women accomplices would contrive com- promising situations in which they and their admirers might be advertently discovered. The most reliable authorities hold that this was never the case. The seduc- tions described in the affidavits may not have been genuine seductions, the element of beguiled innocence being absent in most cases, nor is it likely that many real promises were breached; but it is doubtful if any of Hummel's victims ever paid for an adventure he had not had. In fact, George Gordon Battle, another lawyer who occasionally represented a victim of the racket, maintains that in many cases there was a kind of rough justice in the penalties Hummel imposed. "It was an exceedingly low business," Battle said recently, "but I'll have to say this about Abe: I never heard of his framing anyone, and I never heard of a case where the girl didn't get her half. Also, I don't think there were many cases in which there wasn't something to be said for the girl's side of the story. What Abe got was pure blackmail money, but it didn't seem to me too unjust that the girls should get what they did out of it."

Hummel's victims sometimes became his clients. This happened in the case of Stanford White, who, after twice being forced to pony up, decided that it would be sound economy to pay Howe & Hummel a regular retainer to keep down his expenses. Hummel tried to blackmail young John Barrymore, but Barrymore was blackmail-proof. He would put no price at all on virtue. He got to like Hummel, though, and the two became friends. Hummel became his lawyer, drawing up his contracts with managers and counseling him in his first divorce. But it was only on rare occasions that Hummel met the man he was shaking down. Generally, he would notify the lawyer first, saying that he was in possession of an affidavit whose contents, if made public through a suit at law, would be likely to damage the good standing in the community of the client named therein. It was understood that, upon receipt of such a notice, the lawyer was to get in touch with his client and talk over money matters. The precise sum was settled in talks between Hummel and the victim's lawyer. "He was always pleasant enough to deal with," George Gordon Battle says. "He'd tell you right off how much he wanted. Then you'd tell him how your client was fixed, and the two of you would argue it out from there. He wasn't backward about pressing his advantage, but he wasn't ungentlemanly either." Hummel tried to make the day of the final settlement an occasion for good cheer and fellowship. He would have drinks set up in his office, a humidor of good Cuban cigars on his desk, and a fire burning in the iron brazier. When the payment, always in cash, had been handed over to him, Hummel would fetch from his desk all copies of the affidavit and hand them to the victim's lawyer for identification. If, for some morbid reason, the client wanted the papers for his files, they were his for the asking. Most of the time, however, the client wanted nothing more than the permanent destruction of the papers, and Hummel, sympathetic to this line of reasoning, would oblige by tossing them into the fire with a gesture of handsome magnanimity. As the affidavits, which were hotter before they struck the flames than afterwards, burned to crisp, waferlike ashes, Hummel and his guest would toast one another in excellent whisky and pass an hour or so talking lawyer's talk.

Though always hungry for tribute, Hummel could be understanding and even accommodating in the matter of payment. Terence McManus remembers the story, relished for years by lawyers who had dealt with Hummel, of a man who had somehow been warned in advance that Hummel was about to strike. "This fellow was the only one who ever beat Hummel at his own game," McManus recalls. "He heard from someone or other that he was in for it, and he got ready. He called in his lawyer and his accountant, and the three of them sat down and worked out a whole set of books showing that the man was bankrupt and then some. The lawyer was then in a position, when Hummel made his demands, to say that his client, who of course would have considered himself in a tight spot if he ever got down to a million dollars, had been wiped out and that he could prove it by the books. He took the books down to Abe's office, and Abe, who had been sure there was a catch in it somewhere, studied the books for a few days, and then told the lawyer that he was terribly sorry to have bothered anyone in such a bad fix."

Once Hummel offered a kind of professional cut-rate to a fellow-lawyer. "This one is on me," the fellow-lawyer, now one of the best-known in the city, said the other day, "and it will give you an idea of how far into the woods he'd go to set his traps. I was very young at the time and real small fry for a man who had been shaking down millionaires. But I knew what his game was, for I'd made several trips down to the dumpy little office to get the bad news for our clients. Then, by God, one day I had to go down and bail myself out. He was doing a job on me, too. He had it all down in black and white from a singer I'd seen something of a year or so before. Abe was friendly enough about it, as he always was, but insistent. I pointed out to him that I was young and that I was just getting started as a lawyer myself. I just didn't have ten thousand, and five thousand would have ruined me. He thought it over a bit, and after a while he said he guessed it was a dirty trick. He said he'd be willing to forget the whole thing if I'd just help cover time and expenses. It cost me $500 or $250, I forget which."

It was a matter of both principle and good business with Hummel to see to it that a man who had once been successfully blackmailed was never again troubled by the same girl. Of course, if the man was lightheaded enough to be overcome by the charms of another demanding young woman, that was his own lookout, and Hummel would see to it that the girl's interests were well represented. But as far as he was concerned, it was a matter of a single bill for a single seduction. Naturally, it sometimes occurred to the brighter young women that it would be sound economy to make an old investment pay off a second time if that were possible. They would start proceedings through another lawyer. As soon as Hummel heard that one of his victims was being troubled again, he straightened things out for the victim in short order. According to George Alger, of the old and respected firm of Alger, Peck, Andrew, & Rohlfs, Hummel once explained to a group of friends how he managed this. "Before I hand over her share," Hummel said, according to Alger, "the girl and I have a little talk. She listens to me dictate an affidavit saying that she has deceived me, as her attorney, not believing that a criminal conversation [one of the period's legal euphemisms for an act of adultery] had taken place, that in fact nothing at all between her and the man involved ever took place, that she was thoroughly repentant over her conduct in the case, and that but for the fact that the money had already been spent she would wish to return it. She signs this, and I give her the money. Whenever they start up something a second time, I just call them in and read them the affidavit. That does the trick."

Hummel's technique in divorce cases, which was considered an outrage at the time, would be conventional enough today. Perjured testimony, private detectives, and a lighthearted attitude toward the spirit of the law characterized his work. In New York, where the law, then as now, was fairly stringent, he got his divorces, in the main, through collusion, generally with the aid of professional co-respondents. He actually tried to build up business by pointing out publicly how easy it was to get divorced, and the 1902 revisions of the New York divorce laws, which forbade divorce lawyers to advertise, was said to be one result of his flippant and notorious practice. A good part of his divorce business was conducted not in New York but in states where the laws were more liberal. Indiana and Illinois were the easy-divorce states in the eighties, and Hummel had split-fee arrangements with lawyers there. South Dakota was the Nevada of the nineties, and Sioux Falls was its Reno. Howe & Hummel sent whole trainloads of marital malcontents to Sioux Falls. "Journey Dakotaward," Hummel wrote in a signed article in the *Herald* in 1894, "to have the chains quickly severed. Matrimonial fetters are easily shaken there. They have the greatest bargains ever offered in civilized communities. They have fourteen separate and distinct grounds for divorce. Step up quickly and make your own selection. If you like the community, you can remain. If not, ninety days is sufficient."

As a lawyer of low practices and as a known blackmailer, Hummel was frequently deplored and regretted in newspaper editorials, in sermons, and in the speeches of reformers. In 1904 and 1905, when William Travers

Jerome, then District Attorney, was gunning for him, Jerome and his young press agent, Arthur Train, besieged the press with statements describing Hummel as "a disgrace to his profession" and "a stench in the nostrils of the community." The bar, however, bore its disgrace uncomplainingly, and the community did not seem to mind the odor very much. Both Howe and Hummel had been disbarred for brief periods in the early seventies, but during the height of their fame, from about 1875 to 1900, no efforts were made to cleanse the profession of them. "Howe and Hummel were acknowledged rascals and their practice a racket," Martia Leonard has written, "yet they were regarded with a kindly tolerance by their contemporaries. Why? Was it humanity's gratitude for being amused?" That was probably it. As for Hummel, he was, far from being a pariah, a ubiquitous and exceedingly popular figure in O. Henry's New York. "Little Abe, Light of the Tenderloin, first lord of the racetrack, friend to all Broadway," one anonymous rhapsodist wrote of him around the time of his imprisonment for criminal conspiracy in 1907, and the public, excepting its bluenose members, apparently thought of him in those affectionate terms. The very newspapers that condemned him editorially had to satisfy their readers' appetite for news of his doings. He was liked, too, by a good many people who knew him at close range. "It was difficult not to like him," Samuel Hopkins wrote not long ago. "He was gay, meticulous in dress and manner, and always perky as a wren. He was friendly and generous, and somehow or other he always seemed to exude cleanliness, though not of course on the ethical side." Even Jerome, who was sworn to destroy Hummel and spent two years doing so, was not badly disposed toward Hummel as a human being. Once he succeeded in convicting and disbarring him, he got him a sentence so light that a good many of Jerome's backers thought they smelled a rat.

Before his imprisonment, Hummel was a celebrity on several fronts. He was the city's leading first-nighter and one of the most stable fixtures at its race tracks, prize fights, and fancy restaurants. The parties he gave for sporting and theatrical people in his bachelor home, a brownstone in West Seventy-third Street, were reputedly the gayest and most elaborate in town. He was famous as a free-and-easy spender and a bold gambler. With his suits of bank-teller black encasing his tiny body; his enormous head with a derby most unrakishly perched square on the top; and his unceasingly grave and noncommittal expression, he looked more like a truncated mortician than a *bon vivant*. He was a noted *bon vivant*, nevertheless. The papers regularly featured pictures of him in his box at the opera, in the front row of theatres, and posed with Lillian Russell or Lily Langtry, half-encircling their bodiced waists with a spindly arm. When tickets for one of Miss Russell's famous openings at the Casino were auctioned off among her admirers, Hummel proved himself among the five most ardent, with a bid of two hundred dollars a seat for three seats. Everything he did made the newspapers. When he went swimming in salt water for the first time in his life, it was good for a jovial column in the *World:* "Little Abe Hummel Takes First Sea Bath," the story was headed. The sea bath was at Long Branch, where Hummel owned a summer home and where he broke the record for high pinochle stakes by betting two thousand dollars on a single hand. This also was good for a column more or less in all the papers. Hummel owned another summer place in Saratoga, where he was looked upon as a leader of the New York colony. He was the *Herald's* track correspondent during the racing season and an authoritative source of information on the ways of the fast set. "In order to get a comprehensive and impartial view of Saratoga as it is," the *American's* society editor wrote one day during the 1893 racing season, "I called today on Mr. Abraham Hummel of the metropolitan bar." He got a comprehensive story, though not necessarily an impartial one. Hummel said that it was too bad "that the glorious temples of chance, due to Senator Brackett's efforts at futile reform, have had to take to the outskirts of the city," that Jack MacArthur was the handsomest man in Saratoga that season, and also had the largest collection of jewels, and that William F. Howe, "the greatest of all criminal lawyers," seemed to be enjoying the races with his wife and daughter.

The intelligentsia, fascinated as always by the successfully corrupt, cultivated Hummel and made *mots* about him. "This is Abe Hummel, the divorce lawyer," Rennold Wolf, a celebrated wit of the period and later the author of several *Ziegfeld Follies*, once said, introducing Hummel as a speaker at a literary banquet. "You all know Mr. Hummel. When he finds a rift in the lute, he widens the rift and collects the loot." Hummel himself was the author of a good many gags and wisecracks. The very designation of the midtown section as the Tenderloin was his. A police inspector known as Whiskers Williams had just taken over the West Thirtieth Street Station. Williams wandered into Delmonico's one evening and saw Hummel at dinner there. "You'd better behave yourself, Mr. Hummel," he said, with a flatfoot's notion of joviality, "or you won't be coming in here for any more of them juicy beefsteaks you're always eating." "Speaking of that, Inspector," Hummel said, munching on, "that's a pretty juicy tenderloin they just handed you." From then on, Williams spoke of his district as the Tenderloin. "Roosevelt," Hummel once said, referring to the twenty-fourth President, who was Police Commissioner at the time, "Roosevelt—when they bury him, they can write on his tombstone, 'Here lies all the civic virtue there ever was.'" Once, when told that a lawyer who was opposing him on some matter or other had boasted that he now had Hummel in his pocket, Hummel said, "Then he's got more brains in his pocket than he ever had in his head." Asked a question about fees—a matter he and Hummel never discussed publicly, except in terms of general principles,—he said, "You know the motto of our clients: Millions for defense but not one cent for tribute." He was vain about his epigrams. He claimed that it was he and not Joseph Choate who had first observed that there were two kind of lawyers, those who knew the law and those who knew the judge. "Mr. Choate has always been my beau ideal of a lawyer," Hummel said, in 1896, "but it so happens that I made that observation myself many years ago. In fact, I think I made it before I was admitted to the bar myself. I was very observant."

Hummel was an odd combination of probity and rascality. In his criminal, divorce, and breach-of-promise practices, his activities were such that his name has become, among lawyers, almost a synonym for crook and shyster. But there is never so much as a hint of corruption in his record as a theatrical lawyer. His personal devotion to the theatre was so great that he took it upon himself to make what was probably the first thorough study of theatrical law ever made in this country, and for twenty years he had no rival in this specialty. His love for stage people and the stage was absolute and undiscriminating. "Abe Hummel," a contributor to *Valentine's Manual*, a now defunct almanac, once wrote, "invariably appears for the defense. No matter how many ideas the manager has stolen, or how horribly the Queen's English is being murdered, he always makes a plea for the prisoner at the footlights and usually succeeds in persuading at least twelve persons in the audience that the play is not half as bad as it looks."

Sometimes Hummel could not control his own enthusiasm. "The moment he heard or saw something he liked," Will Klein, now a lawyer for the Shuberts, who recalls Hummel from his own early days in theatrical law, recently said, "he'd stand right up in his seat and start clapping and shouting. Every manager in town told his ushers to ignore any disturbance that Hummel might make. If anyone else cut up during a performance, he was thrown out, but Little Abe could clap and shout 'Bravo!' as much as he pleased." He got to be a kind of official booster for the American theatre. "I had a wonderful time abroad," he told a *Herald* reporter when he got back from a trip to Europe in 1901. "A simply delirious time. I visited the races and the great watering places and Antiwich, Mr. Croker's magnificent home in Wantage. What appealed to me most, though, was the triumphant progress of our stage throughout the world. Even Paris is bowing to New York. American vaudeville artists are performing to overflow audiences there, and the *Belle of New York*, a play fashioned according to Gallic ideas of American ways, draws great crowds to the Moulin Rouge. The Paris Grand Opera features two American singers, Mlle. Noria, known here as Mlle. Ludwig, and a debutante, Mlle. Lillyin London. Suzanna Adams, a distinctly American coloratura soprano, is at Covent Garden."

Nearly everyone involved with the American stage, or with any other part of the entertainment world, employed Hummel as attorney. He was P. T. Barnum's lawyer, and he was the lawyer for the Hutchinson & Bailey Circus; when the two were merged into the Barnum & Bailey Circus, he negotiated the deal and drew up the legal instruments. He was counsel to the new circus as long as he continued practicing law. Almost every first-class entertainer in the country entrusted his contract problems to Hummel. He is the lawyer generally given the credit for persuading the American courts that theatrical contracts were valid and their provisions enforceable. Before his time, the courts had tended to look upon actors and managers as people so flighty and irresponsible, and their business so dependent on such intangibles as artistry, genius, and inspiration, that their agreements with one another could not be considered bound by the rules laid down by courts of equity. In a series of notable cases, the best known of which was *Rice* v. *d'Arvile,* in the Massachusetts Supreme Court, when Oliver Wendell Holmes, Jr., was

Chief Justice of that state, Hummel won decisions that established show business as an industry with as much legal status as shoe manufacturing. He represented most of the French and British playwrights whose works were so popular—because, more often than not, they could so easily be pirated—in this country at the turn of the century. He was Thomas Forbes-Robertson's American attorney, and he was attorney to Rostand, Daudet, Richepin, and other members of the French Society of Dramatists, whose official representative he was.

He did all sorts of odd jobs for his theatrical clientele. In 1904, representing a group of managers against a combine of ticket scalpers, who were represented by the young Max Steuer, he won a decision upholding the right of the managers not to honor tickets bought from speculators. His practice reached into every phase of theatrical life. He represented Lillian Russell in divorce proceedings; fought the censors for the burlesque wheels; lobbied for the circus and the vaudeville producers against a bill which would have prohibited the wearing of tights in public. He represented stage people as diverse as Little Egypt and Mrs. Fiske, Modjeska and Ned Harrigan, Tony Pastor and George Lederer. Although Hummel's theatrical practice appears to have been thoroughly respectable, there were occasions when he could not resist introducing Howe & Hummel methods. One such occasion was in 1896, when it became his duty to bring suit against David Belasco for what Hummel claimed was Belasco's unauthorized production of Richepin's *Zaza;* instead of serving papers on Belasco at his home, his office, or backstage, Hummel bought a front-row ticket for one of his servers and had him vault the stage a split second after the first entrance onstage of Mrs. Leslie Carter, the star. Mrs. Carter met the applause of the audience and the outstretched hand of the process server at the same moment. The incident upset the temperamental Mrs. Carter so much that she had to retire for several minutes, summons in hand, and begin all over again.

From time to time, Howe & Hummel struck a blow for human freedom. For the most part, their cases, though often spectacular and sometimes unique, were of little social or political significance, but sometimes, inadvertently, they found themselves on the side of the angels. Their hospitality to the antisocial elements of the community brought them in contact with a good many cranks and a few prophets, as well as with killers and plunderers. For a fee, they would defend liberty as readily as homicide. They protected the right to speak of a woman who went around the country maintaining that she had been driven crazy by the Republican Party, and they were counsel to Johann Most, the head man of American anarchism, when Most was tried for unlawful assembly in 1886. Even in their straight criminal work, they sometimes achieved results beneficial to liberty. Many of these came to pass in their contests with Anthony Comstock, with whom they, as representatives of the most disreputable forces in the city, had a good many brushes. Generally, they licked him.

They defended the right of women to wear tights on the stage and of men to gamble their money away, if that was their pleasure. They defended Olga Nethersole for kissing her leading man with something more than sisterly affection in Daudet's *Sapho*. On one occasion, Hummel stopped Comstock from padlocking a popular resort known as the Midway Plaisance at Grand Central Palace. The place had been featuring a Danse du Ventre, or belly dance, by three Philadelphia Egyptians called Zora, Fatima, and Zelika. Reports of the performance had reached Comstock, and he had the girls arrested. After long hearings in the magistrate's court, the case was dismissed and Comstock was reprimanded as an interferer. The court records do not tell which of the two points in Hummel's argument moved the judge to his decision. Hummel's first point was that the dance on exhibition at the Midway Plaisance was part of an ancient ceremony which devout Moslems like Zora, Fatima, and Zelika were bound by their faith to perform. The second point was that Comstock erred in describing the dance as a "lewd and lascivious contortion of the stomach." The stomach, Hummel said, was nothing but a small sac in the abdominal region whose contortions, if any, could not be perceived except from inside the body. The girls took the stand and testified under oath, an oath which Hummel had made certain was binding, by securing a copy of the Koran for the girls to swear on. "Mr. Hummel mentioned Allah, the deity of the Mohammedans, several times in his summation," the *Herald* said, "and each time he did so the three young women looked reverently toward the East, as is the custom with members of their faith."

When Howe & Hummel had a good censorship or civil liberties case on their hands, they could conduct a defense in the best manner of a Morris Ernst or an Arthur Garfield Hays. They did this in what was probably the most notable censorship trial of the century. In 1873, they were counsel to Mrs. Victoria Woodhull, the great spiritualist, feminist, lady broker, and candidate for President on the Equal Rights ticket, who, along with her sister, Tennie C. Claflin, had been indicted for alleged obscenities in their weekly paper, *Woodhull & Claflin's Weekly*. The eccentric sisters, children of some snake-oil venders in Ohio, protégés of Commodore Vanderbilt on Wall Street, believed that marriage was an obsolescent institution, and to expose it as such they had published in the November 12, 1872 issue of their newspaper a rather meaty account of the Rev. Henry Ward Beecher's supposed affair with Mrs. Theodore Tilton, the wife of a prominent journalist, and a description of the even more supposititious seduction of two underage young ladies at the French Ball, by Luther V. Challis, a married and well-known dealer in stocks and bonds. For reasons best known to themselves, neither Beecher nor Challis would sue for slander, so Comstock had Mrs. Woodhull and Miss Claflin indicted for obscenity, specifying in his complaint that the indecent words were "token" and "virginity." Sale of the *Weekly* was stopped, and the sisters hired Howe & Hummel as their attorneys. Howe handled the case in a manner that has a genuinely contemporary flavor. He made it into a free-press campaign and introduced the familiar camel's-nose-under-the-tent argument. "Intolerance is on the march," he said. "If we lose this battle, who knows but what the Holy Bible, Shakespeare, and Lord Byron will share the fate of this suppressed journal." "Today," said the *Herald*, "Lawyer Howe wore plaid pantaloons, a purple vest and a blue satin scarf on which an enormous diamond caught and reflected the gorgeous rainbow. Thus garbed, he began his inquiry by asking if Deuteronomy and Fielding were obscene, and he asked why the court had not issued an order for the seizure of all copies of the works of Smollet and Lord Byron." While pursuing this line, he harrassed Comstock in three days of what must have been highly amusing testimony. The records of the examination have long since been destroyed, but Comstock's diary contains pained references to his ordeal. "Their counsel were very anxious to break down my testimony," he wrote on January 11, 1873, "but failed utterly. Truth was too much for them. They do not take stock very largely in that commodity." The following day: "Conscious that I am right, I care not. He [Howe] can do me no harm. I ought to blush that I even notice him here." Still, he gave himself further cause for blushing. "They still continue to abuse me," he wrote on January 14, "but they are beneath my notice. Tombs shysters. They are all for free love."

Howe won the case after a summation that would have done credit to a founding father: "Oh, Liberty," he said, "where are thy defenders, Oh, Tyranny, are we to be again subjected to thy sway, that such an outrage can be perpetrated without even the pretense of legality? And is there no voice outside of those who suffer which dares raise itself to denounce it? Verily the days of Republican institutions are drawing to a close. Must it be as the poet says,

> *Truth forever on the scaffold*
> *Wrong forever on the throne?*

The sisters were acquitted and went on to greater glories, as members of Karl Marx's Communist International, as spiritualist leaders, and as early suffragettes. Howe, though, could not champion martyrs indefinitely. As a result of his retention by the sisters, he was also retained by George Francis Train, an eccentric of even broader scope than the Woodhull girls. Train, a

wealthy Middle Westerner who called himself The
Champion Crank, had led one of the oddest American
careers of the nineteenth century. He had been a
banker; a railroad speculator; a friend of the Queen of
Spain, from whom he is said to have borrowed the
money to build streetcar lines in Liverpool and London;
the proprietor of an Omaha hotel; a grubstaker in the
California Gold Rush; a friend of Bakunin, and of Karl
Marx; and an author of popular travel books for boys.
In middle life, he devoted himself to revolutionary
causes, and when the sisters were arrested for their ad-
vocacy of free love, he promptly got himself arrested
for the same thing. He made speeches in their defense
on Wall Street and reprinted the objectionable articles
in pamphlets. Comstock nabbed him, too, and had him
jugged in the Tombs. Howe began to work on Train's
case after he had freed Mrs. Woodhull and Miss Claflin.
Instead of making a free-speech fight, he decided on an
insanity defense. "In his speech in behalf of the defendant Train," the *Sun* reported, "Lawyer Howe made
the point that there were no obscenities in what the
defendant had said or caused to be printed and that if
there were any obscenities Mr. Train was not to be
found guilty because he is insane." The court was impressed with this line of reasoning and offered to release
Train immediately. But Train was not impressed. He
stood up in court and said that he would sooner rot to
death in jail than take so hypocritical a way out. "Take

me back to the Bastille," he shouted to the court attendants. "Away with me to the donjon." His wish was
granted. He was taken back to the Tombs, where he
languished for almost a year, but where he enjoyed
himself immensely by writing poetry for the revived
Woodhull & Claflin's Weekly and where he got himself
elected president of the Murderer's Club. "I'll raise hell
in this Egyptian sepulcher," he would shout to the
guards. Every so often, the court would order Train's
reappearance before it, and Howe would wearily rise
to advance the thesis that his client was out of his mind.
"Back to durance vile," Train would bellow, and back
he would go. Finally, the guards put him in solitary
as a means of getting rid of him, wearing down his
enthusiasm for jail life. It worked. Train reconsidered
his position and notified the court that he would accept
its offer of release. "My lawyers did not understand
me," he told the press when he got out. "They are like
all lawyers. They think it better to lie your way to freedom than to suffer for the truth."

Howe and Hummel were never above encouraging
new crime as a means of creating future business for
themselves. In 1888 they wrote a book which had
exactly this for its purpose. The book is, all things
considered, a remarkable contribution to the national
literature. Its title in full is *In Danger, or Life in New
York. A True History of a Great City's Wiles and*

Temptations, and it is signed "Howe & Hummel, the Celebrated Criminal Lawyers." Written somewhat in the fashion of the *Police Gazette*, which exposed the lasciviousness and corruption of metropolitan life in such a manner as to make them all but irresistible, *In Danger* professes a high moral purpose. It is prefaced by the pious declaration that it was written out of the authors' conviction that, in the words of a clergyman whose sermons had moved them both, "It had been well for many an honest lad and unsuspecting country girl that they had never turned their steps cityward nor turned them from the simplicity of their country home toward the snares and pitfalls of crime and vice that await the unwary in New York." These words, which are almost the first in the book, are the last to be addressed to the honest and unsuspecting. The rest are for the dishonest and suspecting, and the book is in fact a kind of Real Estate Board brochure apprising out-of-town criminals of the superior facilities offered by New York and of the first-class legal protection available on Centre Street at "what we may be pardoned for designating the best-known criminal law offices in America."

It is possible to imagine a thief of the nineties coming to New York from Boston, say, or Philadelphia, with a copy of *In Danger* to keep up his enthusiasm en route, and, later, having the book propped up before him as he jimmies a safe or practices palming gold watches at home. Whereas the *Police Gazette* was merely titillat-

ing, *In Danger* is instructive. First it entices the larcen-
ous with mouth-watering descriptions of the city's
"elegant storehouses, crowded with the choicest and
most costly goods, great banks whose vaults and safes
contain more bullion than could be transported by the
largest ships, colossal establishments teeming with diamonds, jewelry, and precious stones gathered from all
the known and uncivilized portions of the globe—all
this countless wealth, in some cases so insecurely
guarded." Then it tells in gratifying detail, how in this
wonder city "all the latest developments in science and
skill are being successfully pressed into the service of
the modern criminal." It describes the workings of a
dozen skin games, gives the mathematical formulas for
rigging the odds on horses and cards, and explains the
methods of the most successful jewel thieves. It offers
what is probably the most thorough and technically reliable discourse ever written on "the traveling bag with
false, quick-opening sides," "lady thieves' corsets," and
"the shoplifter's muff." Workable instructions are given
for the home manufacture of all sorts of burglarizing
equipment. The book enables any halfway intelligent
reader to make a shoplifter's muff by ripping the stuf-
fings out of an ordinary one and inserting a wire frame.
"With one of these muffs," the authors say, "shoplifting
is so easy as to be successfully practiced by novices."
"In no particular," they go on, "can the female shoplifter be distinguished from other members of her sex

except perhaps that in most cases she is rather more richly and attractively dressed." It is a fairly safe bet that a shoplifter who had read her Howe & Hummel carefully would be indistinguishable from others of her sex, for she would have been well instructed on the importance of neat and conventional dress in working hours, and she would have had an advanced course in spotting store dicks before they spotted her, looking carefully for them in their concealed perches "on seats suspended from the ceilings and in the folds of heavy draperies." Howe and Hummel leave their readers with a low impression of New York detectives generally, and they bring the gladdening intelligence in regard to the regular force that "instead of surrounding thieves with a network of evidence to convict them, the New York headquarters detectives furnish them with all the facilities for escape known to modern criminal practice."

Besides the expository material on every department of crime, *In Danger* contains several chapters on the night life of the city, appraisals of the sort of entertainment to be found at Harry Hill's Dance House, Billy McGlory's, and the French Madame's on Thirty-first Street, where "the performance is of such a nature as to horrify any but the most blasé roué." All this is in the nature of advertising, since Harry Hill, Billy Mc-Glory, and the French Madame were Howe & Hummel clients. However, the main purpose of *In Danger* is self-advertising, and the self-advertising is shameless. The folly of retaining any firm other than Howe & Hummel is illustrated by the story of Harry Weiler, who, after employing Howe & Hummel to defend him for the murder of his wife, had a falling out with his lawyers. Howe & Hummel had gotten Weiler a hung jury on the first trial, and were prepared to go on getting disagreements until the District Attorney gave up. Weiler, however, got uppity and hired another lawyer. He was promptly convicted and hanged. The value of good and steady relations with the firm is pointed up by the case of Maria, a girl who worked Boston night boats both as a prostitute and a thief. Maria's work was perilous, and she was frequently caught. However, she never "let her indignation get away with her but kept quiet and employed Counsellor Howe to defend her." Maria was probably a fictitious name, for the implication was that she was still profitably on the job at the time of writing. The book gave the details of several injured lady cases with speedy triumph for the lawyers and spot cash for the ladies: "Miss Blanchette retained the services of Howe & Hummel, and proceedings were taken which brought the contumacious Theodore to a very satisfactory fiscal arrangement so far as Miss Blanchette was concerned." "Mrs. Hazard was prudently advised to intrust her interests to Messrs. Howe & Hummel. Mrs. Hazard's lawyers carried all before them like a flood." Howe &

Hummel service was classy—more went with it than mere haggling at the bar: "Lawyer Cook [opposing counsel] looked like Charles the Wrestler waiting for a burly and muscular antagonist. Lawyer Hummel was all brains, and when the judge wanted a light Mr. Hummel handed him a matchbox of a solid virgin gold dug from the California mines by Tony Pastor."

CHAPTER FOUR

DEBAUCHED TILL HIS
TEETH FELL OUT

THE firm of Howe & Hummel reached the summit of its lamentable fame in the eighteen-nineties. By then, its name and reputation, spread broadcast by the *Police Gazette* and other purveyors of the gaudy, were known everywhere. It had been in existence long enough to have acquired tradition and venerability; it was the Cadwalader, Wickersham & Taft of low practice. The nineties were good for Howe & Hummel in spite of the fact that the decade was less hospitable than previous ones had been to the leaders of the city's criminal underworld. The reformers had succeeded to a large degree in breaking up the alliance between organized crime and organized politics. As a result, many

of the better-known highwaymen and vice kings who
had once formed the backbone of the Howe & Hummel clientele were either in jail, like Charles O. Brockway, the counterfeiter, or in voluntary exile, like
Mother Mandelbaum, the fence. But, like most drives
against the underworld, this one had chiefly the effect
of tumbling the big shots from the top of the ladder
and thereby making room for those on the lower rungs.
In trouble, the confidence men, bank robbers, and
dollar-a-broken-arm assaulters who were rising to po-
sitions of leadership in the underworld sought out
Howe & Hummel just as their predecessors had
done.

Then, too, there was murder. Murder is a crime little
affected by the tides of politics, and William F. Howe
had more and better homicides in the nineties than he
had ever had before. The decade that produced Little
Lord Fauntleroy and Anna Held also produced Annie
Walden, the Man-Killing Race-Track Girl; Jim Hol-
land, the Texas Deadshot; Alex Miller, who took a
cleaver to his brother, Robert, the Beloved Butcher
of Cherry Street; and, most notable of the lot, Carlyle
Harris, the frail and brilliant young medical student
from Columbia, whose poisoning by morphine of his
child-bride, Helen Potts Harris, seemed to newspaper
readers in 1892 to be a native product quite as good
in the line of *crime-passionel* as anything that was
coming out of Paris, Vienna, or the imagination of

Oscar Wilde. All of these killers, and scores of others who were defended by Howe in the nineties, captured the public fancy, but none of them was more favored than the great courtroom impresario who was attorney to all of them. The interest aroused by the killers themselves was transitory. They came and went like guest stars on a program whose continuing attraction was Howe himself, "that gaily bedecked elephant," as the novelist David Graham Phillips wrote of him, "careening across the sky," with his princely collection of diamonds; his clothes that were, as another writer said, something from the dreams of an English bookie; and his oratory, as purple as anything from his wardrobe, that was so overpowering that it brought tears not only to the eyes of jurors but to his own as well. Howe's defenses were such good theatre that very often in the nineties the old Bowery Playhouse would contrive an evening's entertainment by acting them out straight from the court records.

Every other branch of the business was flourishing then. Hummel was at the height of his success as a divorce lawyer; the breach-of-promise racket, in those years, was bringing down rich philanderers as effectively as ack-ack fire might bring down low-flying geese. The moldy, cluttered uninviting offices of the firm were the scene of enormous hustle and bustle as the nineteenth century ran out. "Talk about your law factories," one local attorney, a man who started his career as an office boy with Howe & Hummel fifty years ago, recalled the other day, "that was the only one I ever heard of that had a night shift. The doors were open around the clock. You could get a lawyer from Howe & Hummel at four in the morning if you wanted to. Every police court in the city had a cop or a clerk or someone who was being paid to recommend Howe & Hummel to everyone who was pulled in. Of course, in the daytime things were humming every second. The waiting-room benches were always filled, and filled with the damnedest collection of people you ever saw. I've seen Lillian Russell in there surrounded by pickpockets, Tammany heelers, and banco men. Boss Platt was there quite a bit, and so was Croker, and Hungry Joe, the card shark. There were dope peddlers, green-goods men, bookmakers, and any number of queer-looking murder witnesses. There was enough there for a couple of wax museums and a freak show."

The decade that saw the firm at the peak of its success also saw the beginnings of its disintegration and decline. Howe, though his career had been a long one, had gotten his start as a New York lawyer rather late in life. When the partnership was formed in 1869, he was forty-one. In consequence he reached the height of his fame and his powers not long before he reached old age. He tried the last of his many celebrated cases in 1897, when he was sixty-nine. This was the Nack-Thorn-Guldensuppe case in Long Island City. In many ways it was the best of all his cases, and it contained most of the elements for a great valedictory on his part. As things worked out, he lost the case—through no fault of his own—and he never got to make the valedictory, but, still and all, the trial was a fitting backdrop for the old gentleman's farewell. The case can be briefly summarized as a kind of hoopskirt version of the Snyder-Gray case thirty years later. Like that notable murder, it took place in a cottage in Queens, involved the killing of an old lover by a new one, and acted as a stimulant to the circulation of the yellow press. In its literary aspects, the case was even better than the Snyder-Gray epic. For one thing, the principals were a heroic lot, fitted to their roles in a heroic production. All three were large, muscular, good-looking Germans. Augusta Nack, the Ruth Snyder of the triangle, was a woman of operatic contours, handsome features, and volcanic emotions. She was a midwife by vocation. Nack was not her maiden name, but the man who had given it to her did not figure in the case. Herman Nack had been the owner of a Tenth Avenue bologna shop until, as one commentator put it, he developed a Tenth Avenue thirst. Only a few days elapsed between his loss of the bologna shop and his loss of Augusta. Mrs. Nack began to take in boarders. Her first boarder was Willie Guldensuppe, a rubber in a midtown Turkish bath. Willie filled the aching void left by Herman's involuntary departure. Willie was a dream boy. He had a Tarzan build, blond, twirling mustaches, and a still life tattooed on his chest. Willie won Augusta's heart in 1894. The infatuation lasted for about two years. Then Martin Thorn, a barber with dark curly hair and flashing black eyes, engaged Augusta's affections. Willie found himself in the position previously occupied by Nack. He was less obliging than Nack, though, in the matter of stepping aside. Mrs. Nack and Thorn had to kill him. They leased a cottage in Woodside, got Willie out there on some pretense or other, and murdered him one May afternoon in 1897. It was, appropriately enough, one of the most thorough jobs of its kind ever recorded. At the trial, it was shown by the prosecution that when Thorn concealed himself in the second-story bedroom that had been chosen for the job, he was armed with a revolver, a poison dagger, a bottle of carbolic acid, a hammer for braining, a rope for hanging, and a knife for carving. He did not use all of this equipment, but he did fire the gun at Willie three times, pierce his heart with the poison dagger, and decapitate him with the carving knife.

The murder of Willie was unique not only in its completeness but also in the fact that its mystery was solved by a duck. After Thorn had made triply certain that the life was out of Willie, Augusta, with her midwife's knowledge of anatomy, cut him up. She put the limbs and the torso in the bathtub and turned on the water, which was left running until she and Thorn got back from a ferry ride, in the course of which one of them dropped a package containing Willie's head into the East River. When they returned, Willie's remaining members had been drained of their blood, and the blood had run out of the tub with the water. Willie's disappearance had been a matter of police interest—and apparently a matter of insoluble mystery—for several days when a Long Island duck waddled over to the murder cottage and found a bathing pool in the yard. The water which Augusta and Martin had thought would mingle Willie's blood with the city's sewage had burst the drainpipes just outside the house and had formed a small, still pond, ideal for a duck. By the time a duck discovered it, much of the water had evaporated, but all the blood remained. When the duck got home, its white feathers were tinged with red. Its owners reported this to the police, and it was not long before Willie's death had been properly traced to Augusta and Martin.

Howe was Thorn's lawyer. Mrs. Nack retained another counsel, because the pair did not want to admit to an alliance of any sort. Howe could never have hoped for a better case. He was always more eloquent in the defense of the cold-blooded murders of amateurs than the tidy, workman-like jobs of experienced killers.

Moreover, there had always been a strong touch of the ghoul in Howe, and there was plenty here for several hearty ghouls to feed on. The public, too, loved the case. The Hearst-Pulitzer war was approaching its climax at the time, and the *American* and the *World* made a battleground of the Long Island City courtroom in which the trial was held. Each day each paper gave two or three pages to the proceedings. The defendants professed total innocence. They denied that they knew Willie or had anything to do with his life, much less his death. They even denied knowing each other well until it was proved that they had rented the cottage together. Howe carried the burden of this argument, and he carried it splendidly. Indeed, he advanced the theory that there had probably never been any such person as Willie and that if, by some unlikely chance, he had existed, there was no proof that he was not still alive. Augusta had cut Willie's body up into rather fine pieces and the prosecution had never entirely reassembled it. Howe pleaded *corpus delicti*. He argued that there was no proof that the assorted arms, legs, and other members brought into court by the prosecution might just as easily have belonged to half a dozen bodies in the city morgue as to Willie. Willie's head was never found. He might have been identified by the fruits and flowers on his chest, but the tattoo, like the head, was never found, though the prosecution argued, with some cogency, that negative proof existed in the fact that a piece of the chest about the size of the tattoo had been sliced off the torso that was found near the cottage. Still, Howe disputed the assertion that the torso was Willie's, or that there had ever been a Willie. He tried to sell the jury on Willie's fictitiousness by making jokes about Willie's name. At various times during the trial, he referred to Willie as Gildersleeve, Goldensoup, Gludensop, Goldylocks, Silverslippers, and "a creature as imaginary as Rosencrantz's friend Guildenstern."

In the view of most correspondents at the trial, Howe was unquestionably on his way to winning an acquittal for both Thorn and Mrs. Nack when Mrs. Nack confessed. Her confession was the by-product of a conversion. In her cell, she had been visited regularly by a local Presbyterian clergyman; he was not the regular prison chaplain but merely a kibitzing evangelist. One day, according to the reports in the *American*, he brought along his four-year-old son, a pretty, curly-haired boy, who climbed into Augusta's lap and asked her, in the name of both his heavenly and his earthly fathers, to confess to the murder if it was really she who had done it. It was hinted in the *Herald* and the *World* that this whole business was part of a nasty deal thought up by Hearst and sold to Augusta, the District Attorney, and the minister. Perhaps it was; Hearst seemed to have an inside track on the story, getting news of the confession a day ahead of his rivals and later publishing some signed articles by the Reverend Miles. In any case, Augusta confessed, first to the boy and then to the District Attorney. "When that adorable child pleaded with me for the truth," Augusta was reported as saying by the *American*, "I could do no other than tell it to him." The confession, of course, took care of Thorn; he got life, and Augusta got nine years. It was scarcely less calamitous for Howe. The trial was nearing its end when it came, and he was already at work on a summation that would probably have been his crowning glory. After hearing the news, he wrote to Hummel, who was in Paris at the time, a letter that must be one of the briefest as well as one of the most melancholy communications ever to come from a lawyer. "Dear Abe," he wrote, "I had the prettiest case, and here is all my work shattered. I can still prove that they couldn't identify Willie's body and that it wasn't cut up in the Woodside cottage. Now all my roses are frosted in a night and my grapes withered on the vine." He tried a few cases after that, but not many, and none that were famous. In 1900, he lapsed into chronic invalidism. It was said that he had been a heavy drinker and a high liver generally. He was certainly a hard worker. There was no other lawyer of the time who would have made an entire summation, hours long, from a kneeling position, as Howe once did when he thought that his eloquence ought to be supplemented by a show of earnest humility. He had several heart attacks, and then, on September 2, 1902 he died in his sleep at his home on Boston Road in the Bronx.

A year or two before Howe's death, the firm had been forced to abandon its Centre Street offices. The city took the site for a public building. The new Howe & Hummel headquarters were in the New York Life Insurance building at 346 Broadway. Both the building and the address were swankier than the old, but the Howe & Hummel penchant for the dingy was unchanged. Instead of seeking the elevation of at least a story or two, which most lawyers appear to think sets them apart from the ordinary run of trades and service people, Howe & Hummel went from street level to the basement. The New York Life Building was handsome, well appointed, and fashionable for lawyers then, but the best-known and most prosperous of the firms it housed was in the cellar. Howe's death altered neither the name nor the spirit of the office. Hummel went on, as he always had, handling all civil aspects of the practice and certain criminal actions; the bulk of the trial work, and the counseling of homicides and hijackers, which had been Howe's department, were turned over to two of his former assistants, David May and Isaac Jacobson. Hummel was fifty-three at the time of Howe's death, and he probably reckoned himself and the firm good for at least another decade, possibly two.

As things worked out, there were only five more years for both, and most of that time was borrowed. Within a year after reorganizing the firm, Hummel was fighting for his life. He lost in the end, but the end did not come until after he had put on one of the best legal shows of modern history, eluded the hunters for ten months in a spectacular manhunt, undertaken an enormous project in wholesale bribery, and added several new tricks to the shyster tradition.

The Dodge-Morse Case, the journalistic tag for the series of events that led to the destruction of Howe & Hummel, began in 1897 with the divorce of an obscure New York couple and ended, a decade later, when Hummel lost his last appeal and had to go to Blackwell's Island. As it ran its long, geographically attenuated course, many of its events became uncertain and unverifiable; and as it involved the fortunes of a growing number of notable and notorious citizens, the motives of its participants became the subject of continuous and still unsettled dispute. The beginnings, however, were commonplace enough. In 1897, Mrs. Charles F. Dodge, the keeper of a rooming-house in the Park Slope section of Brooklyn, was divorced from her husband, at that time a desk clerk in the Everett House on Madison Avenue and Twenty-second Street. Four years later, she married Charles W. Morse, a former citizen of Bath, Maine, who had come to New York by way of Boston, bringing with him a certain genius for frenzied finance, particularly in the wholesale ice business. The divorce which enabled Mrs. Dodge to become Mrs. Morse was obtained on her application. It was granted in New York courts on the ground of adultery and was uncontested. In this action Hummel had no part. Mrs. Dodge's attorney was William A. Sweetzer. Although Mrs. Dodge, or Mrs. Morse as she became, was the moving figure in the case and although she served as the adhesive element which bound together the lives of Dodge and Morse, and, later, of Hummel, William Travers Jerome, and a number of other people, she was the one principal who cast no shadow at all. Throughout the entire case, she remains as motionless, as characterless, as colorless as a glass of lukewarm water. The divorce proceedings which she instituted were followed by litigation in a dozen courts; she never appeared in any of them, either as witness or spectator. The adventures of her two husbands were spread over thousands of newspaper columns, but it is doubtful if, in the enormous literature of the case, there are a half-dozen paragraphs on her. From what little material there is, and from the lack of more of it, she appears to have been a woman of wholly neutral character, malleable purposes, and an appearance on the dim borderline between attractiveness and its opposite. These characteristics, or non-characteristics, were essential to the development of the case. If she had been anything but plastic in temperament, she could never

[*155*]

have been, in one and the same incarnation, a wife to both Dodge and Morse.

Dodge, the first husband and later the prize of the long manhunt, was as much of a cipher as his wife, but where she lacked character in the sense of distinguishing personal traits, he lacked it in the sense of fiber and purpose. Dodge was a Vermont farm boy who had left home in his early teens and had somehow or other drifted into the hotel business. His life from fifteen to sixty was spent as a peripatetic room clerk, with interludes as a restaurant manager and Pullman car conductor. At the trial of Hummel, in which he was the state's main witness, he gave a biography of himself which takes up several closely printed pages of the record and consists of nothing but the names of cheap hotels, names such as Palace and Occidental, interspersed now and then with the name of a restaurant or a railroad line. He averaged better than a job a year. It is probable that these changes had more to do with a developing moral degeneracy than with the quality of service he offered his employers. Life for Dodge, as later became apparent, was at its most joyous when it was featured by a wide variety of erotic experiences, including a rapid turnover in prostitutes, liquor and dope in abundance, and frequent changes from the lowlife night life of one city to that of another. What possessed him to take a wife, during a brief spell behind the desk of a San Francisco hotel in 1877, is difficult to imagine, but the fact is that he did so. In that year he became the groom of Clemence Chrystie Cowles. The marriage lasted through three or four hotels, but it broke up in Brooklyn a good many years before the divorce took place. Left to shift for herself, Mrs. Dodge started a rooming-house, and it was there that she met Charles W. Morse, whom she married in 1901.

Morse's reasons for marrying Mrs. Dodge are only slightly less difficult to fathom than Dodge's. Morse was in his early forties in 1901 and just past the threshold of a remarkable career in American finance. Wholesale ice was his first line. He had started in a small way in Bath, moved from there to Boston, and from Boston to New York. In New York he established a favorable position for the American Ice Company by the generous distribution of stock to Tammany leaders and other influential persons and gradually extended its monopoly over most of the Atlantic seaboard. The ice trust was to collapse in scandal shortly after his marriage to Mrs. Dodge—and with it the Van Wyck city administration, which Morse had bought up—but he was to follow these operations with equally shady ones in banking and shipping. In 1910 he was indicted by the government for making false entries in the books of the Bank of North America. He was prosecuted by Henry L. Stimson and Felix Frankfurter, convicted, and sentenced to fifteen years in the federal penitentiary. His career ran right down into the thirties. He served only two years of his sentence. In 1912 he was pardoned by President Taft, acting on the advice of a board of army doctors who told him that Morse had Bright's disease. It later appeared that all he had were some of the symptoms, which had been simulated by drinking a mixture of soapsuds and other chemicals. The scandal the pardon provoked was forgotten by the time the first World War came along, and Morse became one of the first of the profiteers, getting the government to hand over millions of dollars to him for the construction of ships in nonexistent shipyards. He died in 1933, but Congressional committees were still discovering evidences of his outrageous operations in 1936. For a man about to embark on such a career, marriage to a nonentity like Mrs. Dodge is probably explicable only in terms of propinquity and convenience. His wife had died a short while before, and he was a widower with four children. Mrs. Dodge was no doubt adequate in the role of housekeeper. At any rate, he married. Two years later, however, something in the arrangement seemed lacking, and he proceeded to rid himself of her.

It was at this point that Hummel came into the case. He received a visit one day in 1903 from an elderly man who affected great saltiness of character and who introduced himself as Captain James Morse, a retired sailing master of Bath, Maine, the uncle of the ice magnate, Charles W. Morse, and the treasurer of several of the Morse enterprises. Uncle Jim, as he liked to be called, explained to Hummel that he and other members of the Maine Morses had been distressed by the marriage of Charles to the flaccid rooming-house keeper and that they considered it in the best interests of both the husband and his children that the union be dissolved. He explained that he understood that Howe & Hummel undertook such jobs and that he wished it to undertake this one, for the execution of which almost unlimited funds were available. He further gave Hummel to understand that the family did not want a divorce. They wanted the marriage broken up by any legal means except divorce for which grounds could be found or manufactured. It must have been plain to Hummel at the time, as it was later plain to everyone else, that this avuncular concern was false and that Uncle Jim was acting as the agent for his nephew and employer. Uncle Jim's own funds, though doubtless considerable, were anything but unlimited, and a man who is dependent on another for his living does not lightly undertake to destroy the other's marriage. The truth of the matter, as it developed later on, was that Charles Morse wanted, when freed of his second wife, to take a third, who was Roman Catholic by faith and who could not have married him if he had been a divorcé.

For a lawyer of Hummel's retrograde morality and advanced resourcefulness, Uncle Jim's problem presented few difficulties. Morse's marriage could be in-

validated by invalidating the divorce that had preceded
it—that is, by making Mrs. Morse Mrs. Dodge again.
This could be done by proving that her first husband
had never been properly served with notice of his wife's
intent to sue for divorce. There were, of course, two
obstacles to be overcome in this plan: Dodge, who had
been served in the Everett House on the night of Oc-
tober 3, 1897, and William A. Sweetzer, who, as Mrs.
Dodge's attorney, had served him. Hummel disposed of
Dodge first. A private detective named Edward
Bracken, an ex-cop who for several years had been
doing odd tailing jobs for Howe & Hummel, took up
the scent in New York and found Dodge in Atlanta,
where he was about to hazard new fortunes as a busi-
nessman. At the moment of Bracken's arrival, Dodge
was busying himself with the last-minute details of
opening a restaurant to be called the Ettowa, of which
he was half-owner. Bracken called Dodge away from
his curtain-changing and menu planning, and told him
that there was five hundred dollars in it for him if he
would leave immediately for New York, where the
famous lawyer, Abraham Hummel, wished an interview with him. Upon receipt of the five hundred,
Dodge left the grand opening of the Ettowa to his
partner and went off with Bracken. In New York,
Hummel offered him five thousand dollars if he would
testify that no notice of the 1897 divorce suit had ever
been served upon him. To be sure, this testimony, if

accepted by the authorities, would make Dodge a married man once more, but Hummel assured Dodge that
there would be no claims for money made against him;
the future of Mrs. Dodge-again-to-be would be under-
written by the Morses. Dodge unhesitatingly agreed to
stay on in New York and perjure himself for the five
thousand; the Ettowa promised no such bonanza as
this.

Dodge had been taken care of in a manner familiar
enough to all the ages. Hummel used a different and
smarter approach to Sweetzer, the attorney who had
served the papers on Dodge. So far as is known, he
had no dealings at all with Sweetzer before the referee's hearing at which Dodge was to testify. Sweetzer
was merely notified that Hummel's client, Charles F.
Dodge, was suing for an annulment of the 1897 divorce
and of the grounds on which the annulment was being
sought. Sweetzer, naturally, went to the hearing to
contradict the testimony to be given there by Dodge.
Hummel, however, showed up for the hearing not with
Dodge but with a man named Herpich, a stranger he
had picked up on a park bench because he was about
the size, height, and weight of Dodge. Hummel and
Herpich arrived before Sweetzer. When Sweetzer got
there, he greeted the referee and Hummel, both of
whom he had met on a dozen previous occasions, and
then extended his hand to Herpich, saying, "How do
you do, Mr. Dodge?" Sweetzer had seen Dodge only

once in his life, six years earlier, and it was natural that he should be caught in such a trap. Nevertheless, his error discredited his testimony in advance. Herpich took the stand to say that he was not Dodge but Herpich, a statement of absolute truth for which he received twenty-five dollars, and he was followed by Dodge, who said he was Dodge, another statement of absolute truth. The referee ruled that Mrs. Morse was now Mrs. Dodge again.

Hummel's trick was ingenious, perhaps even unprecedented in shyster practice, but it was in the Howe & Hummel tradition. The method was similar to that used in a hundred cases before this one. By all the rules, this case should have ended and been forgotten when the divorce was annulled. Everyone but Sweetzer was satisfied, and his loss had cost him nothing. Morse was free of his wife; Dodge had his five thousand; Hummel had more, probably about five times more; Mrs. Dodge-Morse would have had grounds for displeasure if she had not, like her newly regained husband, been bought up in advance; she was, at this stage, living in Paris, presumably on a fat pension. It was Sweetzer's professional pride, a factor which Hummel had understandably neglected to take into account, that led to the next development. Sweetzer was chagrined at having been taken in so easily, and he was determined to seek vindication. He got it without much difficulty. As it happened, back in 1897, Dodge, although he had not contested the divorce, had written his lawyer that he had been served with notice of his wife's intent to sue. Hummel knew about this, but, aware that Dodge's lawyer had since died, he had decided that he would ignore the matter. Sweetzer, however, managed to get hold of the dead man's papers, and he found among them the letter from Dodge. He took it to William Travers Jerome, who was then District Attorney of New York County.

For a moment, now, the Dodge-Morse case flowed into the main stream of American history. The evidence Sweetzer had found had several obvious uses. It was direct evidence, of course, of Dodge's perjury. To anyone who did not accept the fiction that Hummel had been acting as Dodge's attorney rather than as Morse's, it was also evidence of subornation of perjury and related malpractices on Hummel's part. To anyone who could guess, as Jerome certainly could, that Hummel was in fact acting for Morse, it was evidence of subornation of perjury and possible conspiracy on Morse's part. In the end, the evidence was used only against Hummel, whose destruction stood, at the end of Jerome's two terms in office, as the greatest single coup of his administration. It was quite a coup, but it was not the one Jerome hoped for when he saw the prize that Sweetzer had found among the dead lawyer's papers. Jerome was a dynamic and hugely ambitious man, and it had been plain from the moment he took office as District Attorney in 1901 that he had his cap set for bigger things. Theodore Roosevelt, whom Jerome knew and rather scorned as a mediocrity, was President then, and his path to the White House had led through the Police Commissioner's office up the street and the Governor's office up the river. Jerome knew that he had everything that Roosevelt had. He was physically attractive, intellectually powerful, politically bold and at the same time shrewd, and he had good family connections. (Jerome and Winston Churchill were first cousins; Churchill's mother was a Brooklyn Jerome.) He was an open candidate for the governorship, and he was being given a build-up, by the young Arthur Train among others, for an eventual try at the presidency. He got thrown off the track along the way, but a good many historians have since felt it entirely reasonable to speculate on what might have happened in the event that William Travers Jerome and not Woodrow Wilson had beaten Bryan and Champ Clark for the Democratic nomination in 1912.

It was partly, and perhaps decisively, due to a kind of thief's honor displayed by Hummel on the eve of his downfall, that Jerome did get thrown off the track. When Jerome saw what Sweetzer had found, he saw in it not so much the chance of getting Hummel as the chance of getting Morse. Hummel was big game for any district attorney, but Morse was even bigger. By convicting Hummel, Jerome would get the kudos for removing one crooked lawyer from the community—the greatest of all the community's shysters, to be sure, but a shyster nonetheless. The possibilities in prosecuting Morse were endless. Morse was not a mere fool or symbol of corruption; he was corruption personified. He had built his trusts in ice and in shipping by corrupting whole city and state governments. As the president of the Bank of North America, he was at the very center of the whole underworld of crooked finance. Of course, convicting Morse for an attempt to settle his domestic difficulties by conspiring against law and justice would not have had the same value as a conviction for his illegal business operations, but it would have helped. Also, there was probably the possibility of leading from the conspiracy against the marriage laws into a trust-busting operation. To avoid imprisonment, if he were threatened with it, Morse might have opened up on figures still higher in the business world. With such vistas opening up before him, Jerome felt that the conviction of Hummel would be very small stuff. The situation was in a way comparable to the one which Thomas E. Dewey faced some years later when he got the goods on Dixie Davis, attorney to the underworld leader Dutch Schultz and Schultz's errand boy to Jimmie Hines, at that time the center of corruption in Tammany Hall.

Dewey did not prosecute Dixie Davis, the mouthpiece. Instead, he exchanged a promise not to prosecute Davis for Davis' promise to testify against Hines, whose conviction, in 1939, put Dewey in line for all the blessings he has since enjoyed. Jerome planned on doing much the same thing. He planned to exchange a promise not to prosecute Dodge for Dodge's promise to give him the evidence that would convict Hummel. Then he planned to promise not to prosecute Hummel in exchange for Hummel's promise to help him convict Morse.

But Hummel was not a Dixie Davis, and Jerome did not get even as close to the White House as Dewey did. During the next two years, Jerome made Hummel offer after offer in an effort to get him to admit that the Morses were his clients. He made it through the newspapers—"The net, when it is dragged in, is expected to contain leaders in the world of finance," the *Times* quoted a member of Jerome's staff as saying—and presumably he made it often in private. Hummel, however, was not having any. It was a curious kind of conscience that led him to blackmail, to suborn perjury, to buy up judges and prosecutors, to frustrate justice in any way his fertile mind could conceive, and, finally, almost to ruin a man's life, yet stopped and reared back at the prospect of breaking a professional confidence. Indeed, it is doubtful if a professional confidence was really involved. Hummel could have made a deal with Jerome merely by owning to the fact that he had been retained by the Morses. It has always been a moot question as to whether the admission by a lawyer that he is serving a particular client is within the privileged area of professional confidence. But Hummel, like every other human, had to take his stand somewhere. Rather than lessen the value of his pledged word, he risked not only his future as a lawyer but his freedom. Jerome, resigned to the impossibility of getting Morse, began to go after Hummel, whom he finally got.

By the time Sweetzer had uncovered the evidence of Dodge's perjury, Dodge was back in Atlanta with his five thousand. He had given up the Ettowa project for the far more joyous one of getting rid of his Judas money as quickly as possible. When Jerome's detectives went South with warrants for Dodge's arrest and extradition, they found him easily enough by making inquiries in Atlanta's gaudier brothels and hop shops, where Dodge, in the brief few weeks of his life without labor, had made himself known as a steady customer and a heedless spender. He was leading something of a home life, too; Jerome's agent picked him up in a newly rented flat presided over by a Negro mistress named Marie Laws. The detectives escorted him back to New York, where he was promptly arraigned, indicted, and released in ten thousand dollars' bail. The ten thousand was put up by Morse and was the first of a great many such payments made by the Morses to Hummel, who was willing to protect his clients but who insisted that, in return, they finance his efforts to protect himself. The full cost to Morse of Hummel's long struggle against Jerome has never been known, but, in view of the high cost of judges and of the capacity of a man like Dodge for expensive dissipation, the figure could not have been much less than a million dollars, and it could easily have been more. Over two hundred thousand dollars was accounted for when the case·came to trial in 1905.

With Dodge under arrest in New York, Hummel had to see that Jerome did not get to him and buy him out with an offer of *nolle prosequi*. He got another parcel of cash from Uncle Jim Morse (all money, it later turned out, was exchanged by Uncle Jim and a Howe & Hummel employee, so as not to involve either Hummel or Charles Morse, and it changed hands in Stamford, Connecticut, so as to put the act beyond Jerome's jurisdiction) and sent Dodge off to New Orleans with Bracken, the private eye who had originally fetched Dodge from Atlanta. New Orleans was chosen, probably, not only because of its remoteness from New York but also because of its noted facilities for debauchery. At any rate, the detective and his ward registered at the St. Charles Hotel on Prince Street, and spent there the first three months of what was to be, for Dodge, a year of unrestricted, though occasionally interrupted, indulgence.

No other New York district attorney ever fought so hard and against such odds to get his man as Jerome fought to get Dodge. It was three months before he had any luck at all in finding where Hummel had sent Dodge. His own office detectives and those of the Police Department dragged the country and found no trace of him. He solicited the aid of police in other cities, and in most cases got it, but still Dodge did not turn up. The police of New Orleans assured Jerome that Dodge was not in their city, and the New York cops who had been down there reported that, wherever else Dodge might be, he was certainly not in New Orleans. Dodge might have lived out his days, or Jerome's term, at any rate, without discovery if Jerome, despairing of the forces supplied him by the city, had not acquired the services of a private operative named Jesse Blocher, who, for his work on this case, deserves to rank as one of the great American detectives. Blocher, whose reports to Jerome are the only surviving records of the events of this period, went into the District Attorney's service in January of 1904 and, acting either on a hunch or a tip, left New York for New Orleans on January 23. By the 25th he had located Dodge and Bracken in the St. Charles. He found them by means of a simple but clever device. Upon his arrival in New Orleans, he

stopped off in the offices of a broker in railroad tickets
and came out with a handful of the man's rate cards.
He inserted each card in an envelope and wrote Dodge's
name on each envelope. When he entered a hotel which
he thought might be harboring Dodge, he waited before the mail desk until the clerk's back was turned and
then quickly laid one of the envelopes on the desk.
The clerk at the St. Charles, when he turned around
again, picked up the envelope, read the name of the
addressee, and slipped it into Box 420. Blocher left
for an inspection of the fourth floor and found a vacant
room directly across the hall from Dodge. He returned
to the desk and told the room clerk that he had stayed
in Room 423 on a previous visit and wished to rent it
again if it was vacant. He got the room, and he soon
learned the origin of the misleading reports from the
local police. In the steady procession of people going
into Dodge's suite to entertain him or to consult with
his guardian, Blocher spotted a man he knew to be a
high official of the New Orleans force. The Morse
money had been buying the bum steers on Dodge's
whereabouts, just as it had presumably purchased those
of Jerome's own detectives who could not find Dodge
anywhere in New Orleans.

It also purchased a right steer on Blocher's presence,
for the next morning Dodge and Bracken decamped.
Blocher managed to get on the same train with them,
and the next three months were spent in a fabulous

battle of writs. It was master-minded by Hummel and Jerome in New York ("They plotted their moves at tables not ten feet apart from one another in Delmonico's," Arthur Train wrote) and played out by Bracken and Blocher in Texas. All told, there must have been something like a hundred writs of one sort or another issued. The first was sworn out in Houston, where Dodge was removed from the train by local police. Once aboard the train, Blocher had wired Jerome of its destination, San Antonio, and Jerome had got in touch with the Houston police in time for them to catch the train as it passed through. But Hummel was well posted, too. Local counsel for Dodge arrived just behind the police. Dodge was taken into custody, but within a few hours he was free on a habeas corpus. Dodge was rearrested, and again freed on a habeas corpus issued by a judge in another county. And so it went. For every official who would proceed against Dodge as a fugitive from New York justice, there was another who could be talked or bribed into obstructing the procedure. Hummel's resources in legal snafu were endless. Jerome had to swear out three extradition warrants upon the Governor of Texas. Two of them were lost. The first was entrusted to a Sergeant Herlihy of New York's finest. Somehow or other, the sergeant lost his way and had to return. New warrants were issued to some other officers, and they got to Texas, but immediately upon their arrival they met some interesting people, had a gay night on the town in Austin, and woke up in a strange hotel. Something or other had happened to the papers. They couldn't remember the name of the last saloon they had been in. The third actually got to Governor Lanham in Austin, but there were interminable hearings over its legality. Finally, it was approved, but the officer who was about to serve it was himself served with an order restraining him from taking Dodge into custody pending a hearing on a writ of habeas corpus before the United States District Court in the Southern District of Texas. An appeal on another matter was before the United States Supreme Court.

While Hummel was finagling delay after delay, he was making attempt after attempt to get Dodge out of the country. Once, a plan was discovered to take Dodge to the State Fair in San Antonio, disguise him as a lion tamer or a tattooed woman, and slip him into a carnival troupe that was leaving soon for Mexico, and from there for Europe. On another occasion, Blocher somehow got word that Dodge was stowed away on an English merchantman in Galveston harbor. The plan, he learned, was to have him transferred to a seagoing tug that had been leased by Hummel from the Southern Pacific Railroad for the purpose of taking Dodge to Mexico. There was, apparently, no way in which Blocher could remove Dodge from the merchantman, but he did ask the Southern Pacific to order

the tug captain to put in at Brownsville before pro-
ceeding further. The order was issued, but Blocher,
anticipating an attempt to bribe the captain into dis-
obeying, applied to the commander of Company D
of the Texas Rangers to have a detachment meet the
tug at Pont Isabella, at the mouth of the Rio Grande.
Setting a trap which would give him grounds for re-
arresting Dodge, he got the commander to substitute
one of his men for the desk clerk at the Miller House
in Brownsville, where the Dodge party would have to
put up for the duration of the delay. Dodge and
Bracken walked right into it. The Ranger behind the
desk asked them if he could be of any assistance in
helping them with their traveling plans. They took
him up on it, and asked him to get them train tickets
for Monterey. That was all Blocher needed. Dodge and
Bracken had given direct evidence of their intention
to leave the country, and given it unsuspectingly to
an officer of the law; when Blocher reached Brownsville
(he had come part of the way by train, part by stage,
and part by burro-cart express), he and Captain Hughes
of the Rangers arrested both Dodge and Bracken.

Another legal fight began, but it did not last very
long. Hummel got a habeas corpus from a judge in
Nueces County and another from a judge in Bee
County. Police from both those jurisdictions came to
Brownsville to assume custody of the prisoner, but
Captain Hughes refused to give him up, saying that

he was holding Dodge under orders from his commander-in-chief, the Governor of Texas. Hummel then went into Federal Court in Houston, and got an order for Dodge to be given over to the custody of a United States Marshal. Captain Hughes, however, refused to yield up the prisoner even to a federal officer. This turned the fight into something more than a tussle over the carcass of a man wanted for perjury in New York; it was a serious clash of authority among county, state, and federal agencies in Texas. The clash was resolved by a new order from Federal Court in Houston to bring Dodge there under the joint custody of the Rangers and the United States Marshal. In Houston, Dodge was put at liberty on a $50,000 bond, pending the decisions upon the habeas corpus proceedings of the United States Circuit Court of Appeals at Fort Worth and the United States Supreme Court at Washington. After this order had been issued, Hummel did not again try to spirit Dodge out of the country. Dodge was being closely watched now by the police of two cities, two states, and the federal government. It was May when Dodge was returned to Houston, and it was not until December that the legal tangle was untangled.

Hummel failed in his efforts to get Dodge out of the country, and in the end his legal resources were exhausted. He then tried to win with an extraordinary campaign of debauchery. Throughout the long battles in court, Dodge had been having a gay time of it. Every so often, it had been necessary for him to sober up long enough to make a brief appearance in court, and he spent four or five nights, in four or five months, on trains, aboard tugboats, or in jail. But most of the energy in the battle for possession of him had been expended by lawyers, detectives, and police. While they did the spying and the haggling, Dodge spent the money being rushed in daily by the Morses. It was necessary, from Hummel's point of view, not only to see to it that Dodge enjoyed himself, but also to keep him on the move so that neither Blocher nor any other agent of Jerome's could talk with him. If Jerome had been able to reach Dodge, through Blocher or anyone else, he might easily have won Dodge over by the promises of immunity that Jerome was perfectly willing to make and, in fact, fully intended to make as soon as they could get him back to New York. Hummel kept him going so fast, though, that scarcely anyone ever got a word with him, and he kept him so sodden with drink that those few who, like Blocher on one or two occasions, did manage to see him found him completely insensible to reason.

The dissipation Dodge was allowed in the first four or five months, however, was a kind of Quaker soirée compared with what was provided during the last several months in Houston, while Dodge was under continuous surveillance and the word of the higher courts was being awaited. The late Arthur Train, who had access to some of Blocher's reports to the home office, once said that it was doubtful if ever in the long history of human debauchery any one man had ever been indulged with the studied intensity with which Charles F. Dodge was indulged in Texas during the summer and autumn of 1904. According to Blocher's reports, the hours in which Dodge slept in that period were roughly from seven in the morning until nine or ten. Dodge was a frail and nervous-looking man in his middle fifties, but his endurance was seemingly unbounded when he was living the life he liked. The two or three hours' sleep he got along on was had in a Louisiana Street brothel, the fanciest in Houston, which he made his headquarters. He would rise at nine or ten and breakfast on eye-openers. Soon after that he was picked up by Bracken and taken out for the day. Nothing in the bars or bordellos was begrudged him. If it was gambling he wanted, it was to the races he went, accompanied by Bracken with a suitcase full of currency. If it was to be dope, they repaired to the matinee hop sessions. Early evenings, they went to the faro banks and then back to the brothels, either the home base on Louisiana Street or any other that took his fancy. This routine varied as it was Dodge's pleasure to vary it, but it was never interrupted. "It is very hard to keep up with him," Blocher reported to Jerome. "His feet never touch ground."

As this went on, Jerome and Blocher began to believe that Hummel's plan was to kill Dodge by concentrated dissipation. Hummel had all but lost the fight on every front. His case in the higher courts was weak, and pressing it was advantageous only for the purpose of gaining time. Blocher and Jerome charged that Hummel was now trying to wreck Dodge before he got a chance to testify. It may well have been the case that Hummel, knowing that he could not hold Dodge forever, was trying a kind of scorched-earth policy on him. But an equally plausible, and more charitable, view would be that Hummel was forced by the fear that Dodge might go over to the enemy outright to step up his policy of appeasement. While Hummel could not in the long run have hoped to win the legal fight, he could quite reasonably have hoped that at some point he might exhaust Jerome. Besides, District Attorneys do not stay in office for life. Jerome was up for re-election the following autumn. Whatever Hummel had in mind, however, he very nearly succeeded in debauching Dodge to death. He did debauch him until every tooth in the man's mouth dropped out. When Jerome finally got Dodge, he found that his star witness could scarcely talk. He could not get up any volume at all, and what sound he did make sounded as if they came from a man with a mouthful of straw. Before Jerome could put Dodge on the witness stand, he had to buy him a set of false teeth and stand the expense of several other minor repair jobs.

Dodge was in an advanced stage of decay when word from the courts finally came through. On December 3, 1904, the Supreme Court decided the appeal in the habeas corpus against the prisoner. A short time before, the Circuit Court of Appeals had also decided against him. With the Supreme Court's decision, Dodge was put in the custody of a United States Marshal, who had orders to remove him to New York as soon as a few loose ends of the legal fight had been tied off. Hummel made one final effort to get Dodge back. In Wharton County, his agents found still one more who would issue a habeas corpus, and they persuaded the county sheriff to swear in a *posse comitatus* of one hundred men for the purpose of going to Houston and taking the prisoner from the Marshal and his men. One hundred men were actually sworn into this posse and armed with rifles, and Blocher claimed that they had been paid one hundred and fifty dollars each for the job. He believed that the idea was not so much to regain possession of Dodge as it was to provoke a little gunplay with the federal men, in the course of which somebody's bullet might find Dodge. The plan, if that was it, miscarried. The court ordered Dodge taken to Galveston for safekeeping until he could be shipped North. He finally left Galveston on December 16 and arrived in New York on Christmas Eve, 1904.

All the rest was anticlimax, but the anticlimax lasted twenty years. So long as Hummel had been able to keep Dodge and Jerome apart, he had had nothing to worry about. Now that Jerome and Dodge were together, and in Jerome's jurisdiction, Hummel's cause was all but lost. He made only gestures of resistance. The first was on Christmas Eve, the night Dodge was brought into town and locked up by Jerome. As reporters who were there recall it, the scene was one of shiny contrasts. It was a snowy evening, and the hulking Texas Marshals who had come North with the prisoner were watching the wonders of the fall from the windows of Jerome's office, drinking heavily to celebrate the victory and to commemorate the season, and raising general Texas hell in the corridors on the safe side of the Bridge of Sighs. Into this tall forest of ten-gallon hats, the sawed-off Hummel came, dressed in evening clothes and swinging a cane with more jauntiness than he felt. "I'm Mr. Hummel," he told the cop at the reception desk, who knew very well that he was Mr. Hummel. "I have come to confer with my client, Charles F. Dodge." "He isn't your client any longer," the cop said. "He's got another lawyer." Hummel made one more request, a formality. He wanted more than the cop's authority for Dodge's squealing. Word was sent in to wherever Dodge was being kept, and word came back out that Dodge did not want to see Hummel. Hummel left without further exchanges. The reporters followed him back to his home, where his theatrical friends were enjoying one of his gayest parties. The pusillanimous room clerk, apparently, had turned state's evidence within a few hours after his arrival. He kept talking for the next two days, even while he was being sobered up, barbered, and measured for his store teeth. Over the holidays, Jerome gave Hummel several opportunities to do the same. The newspapers were full of variations of the *Mail's* statement that "It may be an error to assume that the Dodge-Morse case will affect high legal circles. In fact, no lawyers at all may be involved, a prosecuting authority said today." So far as is known, Hummel never even discussed going over to Jerome's side. He tried to get the Grand Jury snarled up, but he won himself only a few weeks' delay. Hummel, Bracken, and several other members of the firm were indicted. In the end, though, all the indictments except those against Hummel and Bracken were dismissed. Bracken had been indicted *in absentia*. He had jumped his bail and gone to Paris, where he lived on money, it was said, that Hummel had forced Morse to put up in payment for faithful service. Nothing more was ever heard from Bracken.

Hummel was put on trial in January of 1905 and convicted in two days. It was by far the least dramatic trial that Howe & Hummel had ever had anything to do with. Dodge took the stand to say that his perjury had been suborned by Hummel and that Hummel had financed the flight into Texas. Jerome pulled a mild surprise strategy by putting Nathaniel Cohen, Abraham Kaffenburgh, and one or two other junior members of the firm on the stand as prosecution witnesses. They refused to answer any questions put to them, basing their refusal on the right to avoid self-incrimination. The effect, naturally, was further to incriminate Hummel. Hummel did not testify in his own defense, no doubt because he did not want to give the District Attorney's office the chance to rake over the Howe & Hummel muck of the past forty years. The newspapers had been expecting to get a great deal of this, but they were disappointed. Aside from Dodge's mumbled testimony—he never really mastered the new teeth—there was no interesting evidence. There were, of course, no documents of any kind. Actually, Hummel made no defense at all. When the prosecution had rested its case, De Lancey Nicoll, the former District Attorney and an old antagonist of Hummel's whom Hummel employed to represent him, told the court that he had no witnesses to call and that he wished only to speak to the jury for a short while. He asked the jury to take into account the several reasons of self-interest that Dodge had for testifying as he did. "Poor little Hummel," Nicoll kept calling his client. The jury knew well enough what Dodge's motives were, but it accepted the substance of his story and found Hummel guilty after eighteen minutes. During a recess toward the close of the case, one of the jurors told the judge that Hummel was trying to reach members of the jury with big money. Obviously, he failed to do so; whether or not he tried was never known.

Jerome was not vindictive. Before and during the trial he had affected the pose of a Saint George, but it was only a pose. He was sincere enough in wanting to remove Hummel from circulation, though he would sooner have removed Morse, but he had no particular wish to see Hummel suffer. In the course of the trial, he had the indictment whittled down to one count, conspiracy, and it is said that he privately recommended to Judge Fitzgerald that the judge be lenient in sentencing. In the end, Hummel paid a fine of five hundred dollars and spent a year on Blackwell's Island. All things considered, this was an exceedingly, not to say suspiciously, light sentence, and it was explained to the public that it was light because of a deal Hummel had made with Jerome concerning the Thaw case. Stanford White, a regular client of the firm, had once brought Evelyn Nesbit Thaw to Hummel's office to make out an affidavit against her husband. It was during a period of estrangement from Thaw and infatuation with White, and in the affidavit she swore that Thaw had once told her, in Paris, that he intended to kill White some day. Jerome used the document to establish intent and premeditation on Thaw's part. For identifying the document and testifying to its authenticity, Hummel got a bargain sentence. At least, that was the reason given.

It was almost two years after his conviction that he began to serve his term. Both he and his lawyers looked long and hard for technicalities on which he might avoid going to jail. They found none. On March 8, 1907, Hummel, who in 1872 had helped to spring two hundred and forty prisoners from Blackwell's Island, went there himself. The night before he left he threw the greatest party of his life at his home in West Seventy-third Street. A cordon of police was thrown around the block to prevent any attempt at escape. No attempt was made. Reporters were kept out of the party, and the list of guests was never given out. One reporter wrote, on what authority he did not say, that at midnight Hummel made a farewell speech to his friends, saying that he had been restrained from committing suicide only by the knowledge that he was needed by his two sisters, one a spinster and the other a widow. The next morning he was taken to the Island. The papers played the story for all the human interest they could wring from it. On the night of the party they had described the route he would travel the following morning. Fairly large crowds lined the streets, so the police decided to use another route. The prison authorities put him to work in the bakery, but he did not last long there. He developed some stomach ail-

ment or other, for which he was excused from all labor.
The papers kept a close check on his life as a convict.
He did not wish any publicity, and reporters were
forced into all kinds of ruses to see him. "I may as well
confess," wrote a man from the *World* in a two-column
interview on December 9, 1907, "that I went there
with an artist posing as a student of criminology from
San Francisco. It was the only way to secure Hummel's
consent for a visit. He will not allow anybody to visit
him except those of his own blood, because although
he is sheathed in degrading stripes, he has left in him
much of the vanity that used to cause him to loll up
and down the middle aisles of the leading theatres on
nights of splendor and rejoicing." The *World* man was
particularly interested in reports that Hummel was
enjoying unusual privileges as a prisoner: "One report
had him out on a joyous carouse one night on West
125th Street. Another had him located in Saratoga in
the closing days of the summer. Still another had him
wearing the dandiest kind of handsomely tailored clothing, smoking fragrant cigars, and taking the air around
the Isle de Blackwell whenever the spirit moved him."
Hummel denied every bit of this. "My clothes are tailor-
made all right," he told the reporter, "but the tailors
are evidently short-termers who haven't gotten on to
the graceful curves of Jim Bell or Tom Maguire."

The reporter's visit may not have been the surprise
he thought it was. Charles C. Burlingham remembers

a dinner at Henry Stimson's many years ago. A good many respectable lawyers were there, and De Lancey Nicoll got to talking about Hummel. "He said," Burlingham recalls, "that when Abie was imprisoned on Blackwell's Island he went over there to call on him. Turning to Mr. Root, Nicoll said, 'Have you ever been on Blackwell's Island, Elihu?' Mr. Root said he had not. 'Well,' said Nicoll, 'you wave a handkerchief and a rowboat comes over and picks you up. It is manned by a penitentiary crew in stripes and the keeper sits in the stern with a gun. When we got to the pier on the Island, Abie was there to meet me, and he took me up to his room—a fine and spacious room in the workhouse. I said to him "This must have cost you a lot, Abie, didn't it?" "Yes," he said, "it did." (It was the warden's room.)'" Nicoll, as Burlingham remembers it, went on talking about Hummel with what would seem to have allegorical intent, or perhaps it was merely the spirits flowing. "'I said to Abie, "Now you're disbarred and you won't be able to practice law again around here, I have got a plan for you. I am going to get a good architect to design a nice place for you on Broadway, where you can have a very good time, lots of drinks, nice girls, and everybody will have a wonderful time and over the front entrance will be this inscription, A. Hummel, the man who never squealed." Hummel didn't think well of the plan,' Nicoll said, 'but I went back to town, and I got an architect to make some drawings, and then I took them over to Abie, but Abie would have nothing to do with them. He said he was going to Paris, where he would live with his sister . . .' " The story has the ring of something told by a man in his cups, but the fact that it was conceived and told must have a certain significance. It is a rare thing when the Ladies Aid finds virtue in the town whore.

Hummel's disbarment had followed shortly on his conviction, and the firm of Howe & Hummel was enjoined by law from further practice. A petition to allow its revival, made by Hummel's nephew and partner, Abe Kaffenburgh, was denied in 1909 by the Appellate Division of the Supreme Court. One serious attempt was made to hold on to the firm's prestige and to keep the clientele from dispersing. David May and Isaac Jacobson, who had been Howe's assistants in trial work before his death, started up a successor firm under the name of May & Jacobson. It was a fairly well-known and prosperous firm until the early thirties, but it never towered above its rivals as Howe & Hummel had done. If there was any legitimate heir to the practice, it was Fallon & Magee, the underworld mouthpiece of the prohibition period.

Hummel abandoned all his legal interests in New York the day he went to prison. Within a week after his release, he sailed for London on the Lusitania. The theatrical community sent a deputation to wish him bon voyage. Marcella Sembrich, John Barrymore,

Charles Frohman, and several others were in the group. Flowers and bon voyage messages came from the Earl of Yarmouth, Josephine Jacobi, and Lillian Russell. Hummel made a home with his sisters in Grosvenor Square, but he seems to have spent at least half his time in Paris. He lived elegantly, until 1926, in both London and Paris. He enjoyed himself but was occasionally homesick. "I've been seeing all the plays," he told a reporter in 1910. "The other night I saw Sir Beerbohm Tree in *Hamlet*. It was very nice, but I wish they had something like Joe Coyne over here, and I do wish they'd do the *Merry Widow* this season." No one knows how much of his money he took abroad, but it was probably in the neighborhood of a million dollars. He was as much of a gambler and a first-nighter over there as he had been here, and, after the first war, he became a familiar figure to Americans along the Strand and the Paris boulevards. "I saw him several times in Paris," Samuel Hopkins Adams recalls. "He was wistfully glad to see anyone from his old haunts, even when the acquaintanceship was slight, as it was in my case. He looked as neat and dapper as ever in his morning coat and braided waistcoats. He told me, confidentially, that while he was not practicing in the French courts, he was giving 'occasional private advice' to other expatriates in trouble in Paris." It was said, too, that he augmented the income from his capital by buying into a small chain of Paris movie houses. It

[*187*]

was also said, but on far less credible evidence, that he directed, from abroad, a ring of smugglers who brought contraband jewelry and antiques into New York. A man named Marcus Griffin, who lived at the time in Bernalillo, New Mexico, is the author of a document which asserts that for a while, around 1912, Hummel was living as a well-heeled anchorite in Sandoval County and that he, Griffin, frequently saw him there. His testimony is interesting but not quite conclusive.

So far as is known, Hummel made only one trip back to this country. That was in 1910, when a ship on which he was making a world cruise put in at San Francisco for a few days. He told the reporters that he was at work on his memoirs. Unfortunately, nothing seems to have come of this project. "If Abe Hummel's head should ever split open," Wilburforce Jenkins, a noted journalist at the turn of the century, once wrote, "the secrets that would come out of it would require the publication of sixteen extras a minute for nine years." If he had spilled only a little of what he had learned during his blackmailing days, the book would have been a rare study in urban anthropology. He could also undoubtedly have thrown light on some of New York's famous unsolved crimes. He had been, after all, the lawyer to Mosher and Douglas, who had kidnapped Charlie Ross, whose fate is not known to this day, and to Forrester, the housebreaker who is thought by most experts to have been the murderer of Washington Nathan, the victim in the most famous unsolved murder in New York's history. Howe & Hummel clients back in those days were in the habit of telling their lawyers everything. Whatever plans he had for one day telling what he knew were interrupted by his death. He died in London, in a flat on Baker Street, on January 21, 1926. His body was brought back here. It lay in state at Campbell's Funeral Parlor for a brief spell. Some aging lawyers, cops, newspapermen, and Tammany politicians went up for a look. He was buried in Salem Fields Cemetery in Queens. No one much attended the funeral. All the pallbearers were hired hands. The Howe & Hummel legend, as a piece of vivid but disembodied folklore, thrived in 1926, as it does today, down around the criminal courts, but Abe Hummel, as a public figure had been forgotten by most of New York in an astonishingly short time—in eighteen years, to be exact.

Charles Edward Russell, the old muckraker and Socialist politician, was among the handful of people who showed up for the funeral. Another was a youngish man who took a rose off the coffin, kissed it, and threw it back in the grave. A few months later, when the estate was being settled, the young man showed up in town again and said his name was Henry D. Hummel and that he was the son of Abe and of Leila Farrell, a singer. The young man had grown a mustache like Hummel's to show the resemblance, which was really quite remarkable. It turned out that Hummel had once represented Miss Farrell in a breach-of-promise suit against Nat Goodwin, the great vaudevillian, and that after the suit was won he had set her up in a handsome place on Lexington Avenue. She was his mistress for several years. The young man had a just claim, but he didn't get very much. Hummel's estate was considerable, but that part of it which could be attached in New York County amounted to something in the neighborhood of seventeen thousand dollars. A fraction of this was settled on the claimant, who got a shave, checked out of his hotel room, and went back to his job on a bakery wagon in Portland, Maine.